Praise For

I AM A CHRISTIAN FIRST

Simplified sophistication, is one way to describe this practical go-to resource for Christian C-suite executives and middle managers—and those on the climb to the top of their industry specific fields. In I Am A Christian First, Dr. Stephens highlights how living true to your values is what is required to fill industry-specific leadership gaps. Although the protocols operating in the natural realm are vastly different from those of the spiritual realm, Stephens builds an air-tight case for the superiority of spiritual protocols, in their nature and essence. She provides readers with a practical roadmap for maintaining their distinction as Kingdom citizens while navigating the terrain of the modern marketplace. An intriguing guide full of important tools for those in search of a tried, true, and trail-blazed path to success, I Am A Christian helps readers live balanced lives as they pursue success in an increasingly competitive world.

This book is a must read for anyone whose moral and ethical fortitude demands countercultural strategies. I read this book in one sitting. I couldn't put this page-turning master-piece down.

Dr. Grace Stephens is a brilliant communicator. As you take time to read this extraordinary work, I believe you will walk away rejuvenated and empowered to lead with confidence as a successful Christian professional, as well as live abundantly in every area of your life.

- **Dr. Cindy Trimm**, *CEO/Strategist, Bestselling Author, Humanitarian*

Dr. Grace Stephens has hit one out of the ballpark with this Divinely Inspired Diary that not only offers 12 Success Principles, but also gives professionals permission to be unapologetically and unashamedly Christian First. I wish I'd had this book handy during my tenure at the White House and for the decade I worked in senior government, and throughout my thirty years in private and public sectors. People are so concerned about being "politically correct." This interpretation gives the Believer the right to be Christo-centrically correct.

Dr. Grace's book arrived on a Friday evening and by Saturday morning I was calling her with praise and applause. I read the book from start to finish in one weekend and upon completing it, I immediately gave thanksgiving to God for inspiring Dr. Stephens to write the book. I can't help but think of the many ways in which professionals will embrace this handbook as well as the hundreds of thousands of lives that will be touched by it. From the opening introduction to the closing prayer of salvation, it is filled with Spirit, and filled with her namesake, Grace. I commend it to you highly.

- *Rev Dr. Ambassador Suzan Johnson Cook*, *3rd US Ambassador for International Religious Freedom, faith advisor to two US Presidents, first female Chaplain of the 50,000 member NYPD*

In *I Am A Christian First*, Stephens makes an impassioned and compelling case for the need to redefine what it means to be a professional who is a Christian in today's world. As Dr. Stephens points out, despite the universal positives of a vibrant, selfless faith, the incorporation of spiritual beliefs and practices in workplace settings is still largely unaccepted. Often, working Christians are not encouraged or empowered to practice their faith in the marketplace, so they're fearful about losing their jobs or facing victimization at work – entrepreneurs fear the loss of employees, potential partnerships, patrons, and even revenue if they choose to express their faith and Christian values. For these reasons, many believers tend to leave their faith at the front door of the work setting. By doing so, these "closet Christians," as Stephens so appropriately labels it, fail to advance God's Kingdom for fear of persecution or ostracism.

If you've ever struggled to bridge your faith into your life as a professional, there's hope. In this deeply personal book, Dr. Stephens talks candidly about her successes as well as her own challenges in finding a place for Christ to be revealed and glorified in her career. In a series of crisp and insightful chapters, she offers best practices and actionable techniques paired with biblical principles and powerful scripture-based prayers – all of which are designed to help you navigate common pitfalls and achieve optimal growth as a Christian professional.

- *Tom Nolan*, *COO of TCT Network*

I AM A CHRISTIAN FIRST

I AM A CHRISTIAN FIRST

12 SUCCESS PRINCIPLES FROM
THE DIARY OF A CHRISTIAN CEO

DR GRACE STEPHENS

AUTUMN GRACE PUBLISHING

Published in Chicago, Illinois, by Autumn Grace Publishers.

First Edition

Autumn Grace Publishers titles may be purchased in bulk for educational, business, fund-raising, or sales promotional use. For more information, please contact Autumn Grace Publishers.

Unless otherwise indicated, Scripture quotations are taken from the following sources: The King James Version of the Bible (KJV), The New King James Version (NKJV) and New International Version (NIV).

Cover Design: Grace Stephens, Visionary Designz

Library of Congress Cataloging-in-Publication Data

Stephens, Grace

 I am a Christian first: 12 success principles from the diary of a Christian CEO / by Grace Stephens.
   pages cm
ISBN 978-0-578-80968-7 (paperback)
ISBN 978-1-7923-5562-2 (ebook)
1. Stephens, Grace – Business. 2. Religious Aspects – Christianity. 3. Self-Help & Relationships. 4. Education. 5. Women – Success
                                                          2020923739

Printed in the United States of America

15 14 13 12 11 10 / 7 6 5 4 3 2 1

This book is dedicated to the rising army of professionals whose deepest desire to model Christ and advance the Kingdom of God forms the root of their existence.

CONTENTS

Introduction 17

1. Transcend Fear to Boldness 23

2. When You Fail, Fail Forward 35

3. Walk in Your God-Given Purpose, Not the World's 49

4. Own Your Position, With God's Help 63

5. Pray for Those Who Persecute You 75

6. Watch the Company You Keep 87

7. Work and Lead with Love 101

8. Honor What Others Invest in You 111

9. Use Your Creativity to Solve Problems 125

10. Be Prepared for the Opportunities Ahead 137

11. Achieve Mega Influence by Sharing a Mega Vision .. 149

12. Be a Champion for Christ in the Workplace 163

Conclusion 179

Prayer of Salvation 183

About the Author 185

FOREWORD

When I first met Grace Stephens, she was already a very successful professional, serving as one of America's youngest college presidents. As the president of MacCormac College, founded in 1904, Grace also had the distinction of being the first woman and person of color to serve in that position.

Grace certainly had all of the academic training and professional experience to be a college president. But what caught my attention after she started attending our church, and later our Bible school, was not her professional pedigree. It was her passionate and almost-palpable love for God.

As a pastor and Bible teacher, nothing perhaps gives me more joy than to see others find and grow in their God-given purpose. Grace is a shining example of what I have been teaching for many years. That is, our true identity is who we are in Christ, and our faith and how we serve in the marketplace were never meant to be separated. Whether we work in business, government, education, or some other arena, God has called each of us to influence and shape the world around us for His glory. This book demonstrates that Grace not only understands this but that she is living it.

I am a Christian First, 12 Success Principles from the Diary of a Christian CEO is a real-world handbook filled with biblical principles, practical action steps, and prayers on how to bring your faith to work. Grace is an engaging story-teller who writes from her real-life experiences of being a Christian in the work-place and often at the helm.

I believe many Christians who hold positions of power and influence, or aspire to, will celebrate and identify with her spiritual awakening — from an identity rooted in professional credentials and achievements to an identity rooted in Christ.

This book will encourage and embolden every believer who seeks to find their place of faith, grace, and influence in the workplace.

Bill Winston

Dr. Bill Winston

INTRODUCTION

According to recent data, we spend 13 years and two months—which equates to approximately 4,800 days of our lives—working. Maybe that explains why the first question we're often asked when someone meets us relates to what we *do*.

Before I accepted Jesus Christ as my Lord and Savior, I had a quick and easy reply, since I was the stereotypical professional to whom credentials and achievements mattered a great deal. I had allowed myself to become caught up in a cycle of chasing and achieving one goal after the next, with a focus on working really hard to make things happen. Like many professionals and business owners, I began to believe that my work defined my life.

It can be easy to allow our professional identities to define us in this way rather than seeking and embracing who God created us to be. When this is the case, success itself may become an unintended idol in our lives, preventing us from achieving the plans He has for us.

I've found this to be the case in my own life. Throughout my years of working to hone my professional identity, I intrinsically knew something was wrong. I lacked purpose and experienced an emptiness inside that could not be filled with money, prominent titles, material objects, or social status—all things I already possessed. Over time, I feared that my worldly approach to finding happiness would never amount to anything meaningful and lasting. I suspected there had to be more to life than just building a career.

As a result, I began to seek out and find wisdom from God, instead of the avenues I'd always relied upon. I started to prioritize my spiritual growth by devoting my time to activities that built me up spiritually such as praying and worshiping, meditating on God's Word, serving at church, and practicing financial stewardship. Over two decades, my spiritual life increased exponentially and I eventually learned to identify as a Christian first, rather than focusing on my status as a "professional."

In some settings, combining those two identifiers can be a challenge. Essentially, whether you own a business or work in a small office or large conglomerate, most Christian professionals regularly interact and co-labor with others who are different from us. People whose ideas are divergent from our own. People who believe much differently than we do.

And that's where it can get sticky.

I've found that being both a Christian and a professional does not always lead to harmony. In fact, living out our faith in the workplace can actually be a source of tension and conflict—especially when dealing with those who may not agree with our faith-based approach.

Throughout my career, I've witnessed many difficult dynamics like these. Frankly, the majority of my professional life has involved working in environments with a multiplicity of people with differing personality types and agendas. As a result, I know that individuals in the workplace can be at their very best and at their very worst. Good people can transform into being not-so-good, and meaningful relationships can deteriorate completely.

However, I've also witnessed the redemptive side of that coin in which once-insecure colleagues thrived and became the confident and capable leaders God created them to be. I've seen the transformative power of love and teamwork radically change a person's work style, and integrity-filled leadership completely reshape an entire organization. Such experiences prove that when the workplace dynamic is right, an environment of immense satisfaction can be created.

I've tried to learn and grow as the result of my own experiences on both sides of the coin, also making the most of the collective knowledge and wisdom of others who have been in my shoes (perhaps you're one of them). My desire is to leverage my own leadership lessons and workplace experiences throughout the years into a collective learning of how to balance and effectively manage the tensions between who we are as professionals with who we are called to be by God.

Christ Himself told us those tensions would exist as the result of our identifying with Him. We are also told to "be *in* the world but not *of* the world." Finding that delicate balance and staying true to who God made us to be is the ultimate workplace challenge.

This book is a real-world handbook based on my real-life experiences designed to help you change your paradigm about being a Christian in the workplace. In it, I recount experiences in the work environment in which I interjected elements of my faith and used age-old wisdom to navigate challenging situations. Along the same lines, the biblical illustrations provided demonstrate how certain faith leaders modeled the strength and resilience needed to handle difficult situations in a way that honored God and provided hope where none seemed to exist.

Also covered in these pages are major issues that many face at some point in business, workplace, or personal life. Essentially, these include what I refer to as "The Big 12," which include things like:

- Being bold about our faith
- Working with difficult people
- Reaching our goals effectively
- Failing gracefully
- Leading and working with love

These are just a few of the topics discussed across various sections — which also include scriptural support at the end of each to apply God's infinite wisdom to specific situations.

In addition, points of reflection have been incorporated, as well as written prayers to help navigate readers through some of the more delicate situations they might encounter in the workplace. These additional tools are intended to bring further clarity to these unique situations and provide you with a reminder that God cares deeply about the work you do. He has provided a roadmap to help you successfully navigate the work environment to obtain the bountiful blessings He has specifically prepared for you.

Colossians 3:23 tells us, "Whatever you do, work heartily, as for the Lord and not for people …" The work we do is for the glory of God. Period. When we operate from this understanding, God promises to bless the work of our hands (Proverbs 16:3). He will help us tend to the relationships that need a little more nurturing, and He will help us plot a course toward the best solution in any challenging workplace scenario.

Through this book, my sincere hope is that you will be encouraged and reinvigorated to lead your business and do your work with all diligence and with every measure of excellence to become an effective and successful Christian professional in your business, work, community, and personal life. My prayer is that your faith will be deepened and sharpened in the workplace and that God's mighty power will be manifested through your influence there.

1

TRANSCEND FEAR TO BOLDNESS

David said to Saul, 'Let no one lose heart on account of this Philistine; your servant will go and fight him. ...Your servant has killed both the lion and the bear; this uncircumcised Philistine will be like one of them, because he has defied the armies of the living God. The Lord who delivered me from the paw of the lion and the paw of the bear will deliver me from the hand of this Philistine.'

I Samuel 17:32, 36–37 (NIV)

David wasn't supposed to be a giant killer. He wasn't supposed to be able to ward off wild animals. And he certainly wasn't supposed to be a king. There were a lot of things David was not supposed to do. And yet he did them. It's a good thing he didn't listen to the voices around him—namely, his brothers, his father, a paranoid king, and an irksome giant. David's destiny was dictated by a power much stronger than any of the external forces in his young life.

Everyone loves to recount the famous story of the boy who slayed the giant, Goliath. Every 3-year-old who's ever been to Sunday school can vividly recreate the story of David boldly daring the giant to a fight, and then incredibly felling the oversized bully with a single smooth stone to the forehead. Countless illustrations and interpretations of that story have surfaced through the millennia.

But few people stop to think about the events that took place long before David faced Goliath to become the legend he is today.

> In truth, champions don't become champions
> in the ring—they are merely recognized there.

Likewise, there is usually an event(s) that prepares us for our moment of triumph.

David developed his warrior spirit in an often overlooked passage in 1 Samuel 17:34-36 where he recounts two events from his young past. The first was when the shepherd boy was tending to his flock and a lion attacked. One of the lambs David was watching became the helpless victim of the hungry lion. Distracted by his preparations for what he perceived to be an easy dinner, the lion never saw the blow to the face that came from the diminutive human who was on a rescue mission for his kidnapped lamb. David fearlessly yanked the lamb from the lion's mouth, and when the lion attempted to retaliate, the shepherd boy killed him. But it didn't stop there. When a ferocious bear thought he'd also take a shot at a free lunch at the expense of David's flock, he met the same fate.

David's fearless demeanor wasn't born on the battlefield the day he slew Goliath—it was simply recognized there. When all is said and done, David may not have had the confidence to stand up to the giant if he had not first experienced God's hand in helping him face down the lion and the bear. That's where his faith and mettle were tested—what prepared him for the bigger challenges he would later face.

I can relate to David because even though he was the youngest in his family, he didn't let his age hold him back from being fearless and bold. David developed a very intimate relationship with God while he was still young. He wrote many of the Psalms in the Bible as songs to the Lord while playing his harp. When the prophet Samuel came to David's house to anoint one of the sons to be the next king of Israel, no one even bothered to let David know. Nobody thought he was "king material." But God didn't see a shepherd boy, He saw a king.

When I was a child, my parents had a home in Queens, New York. Every Sunday we went to Brooklyn to my great uncle's house where we would spend time with family. My mother reminds me of the story of when I was just turning eight months old, and was enjoying a birthday party with many of my cousins. I was playing with other babies who were my age, but I seemed more fascinated by the older children who were running and jumping and having so much fun.

According to my mother, at one point I pulled myself up with the assistance of a nearby table, and in the blink of an eye, I was literally off and running around with the one-year-olds. I fell down a few times, but I got right back up as though it were the most natural thing in the world for me to do. Both my mom and dad were shocked at the time, but they were excited to see their first child take her first steps in such an unexpected and daring way. And that became my way of life: I've been running my own race ever since.

When I was around nine or ten, my sister, mom, auntie, and I were at a pool party at our cousin's home in Canada. I suspect our caretakers were having a bit too much fun and weren't really watching us when my curious younger sister decided to go under the divider to the deep end of the pool. I called for help since I couldn't swim, but no one could hear me. So, I figured I had to do something.

I tried to search under the water with my hand while holding on to the edge of the pool, but my sister had floated so far away from me I couldn't feel her anywhere. Finally, I took a deep breath and put my head underwater. She was looking around underwater completely oblivious to the danger she was in. I cried for help one more time, but no one came to rescue us.

Instinctively, I plunged under the water, and pushing off the side of the pool, I catapulted toward her. Then I grabbed her and started kicking my legs as I struggled toward the edge of the pool. When I finally got there, someone saw us and pulled us out of the water. Needless to say, we were scolded, but in my mind, I knew I had saved my sister's life, and I was willing to sacrifice my own to do it. Like David, I was able to instinctively tap into a source of courage I didn't know I possessed at such an early age.

I remember another incident after school one day, when my dad lifted me up and spun me around because I had performed so well in my end-of-year exams I was going to be able to skip the first grade. Back then, I was the smallest in my class, and my mom feared I would be negatively influenced by my older peers or maybe even bullied. My dad asked me how I felt about going to a higher grade, and I boldly stated, "I can do it, Papa." I was fearless as a child.

Fast forward a few years, when my parents were going through a sad divorce. Since I was older than my sister, I felt I had to grow up really fast (my younger brother didn't come along until much later). Rather than playing and enjoying my summers like other kids in my neighborhood, during the summers and breaks in the school year, my mom took me to work with her in New York City where she was a comptroller for a large textile company. If I didn't go in to work with her, she brought work home for me to do.

At the office, I often did billing for her or some other type of work—including filing or answering the phones when the front office person went to lunch or was out on vacation. My mom said it was important for me to learn to work effectively so I could take care of myself and not need to depend on a man to support me. I didn't know it, but even then I was being groomed to become the professional I am today.

When my mom remarried a few years later, life at our house changed dramatically; much of the change was for the better, but some of it was very difficult for me to adjust to. My stepdad was quite strict, so I led a fairly sheltered life and couldn't do many of the things other kids my age did. I wasn't able to go to prom, go to the movies, or hang out with my friends; sleepovers were an absolute no-no. There were basically four places that I frequented: the library, supermarket, tennis court, and church. Everything else was pretty much off limits.

By the time the summer before college rolled around, things had gotten so tense at home that I decided it was time to move out. Although I knew I was risking the loss of financial support for school, I boldly—but not fearlessly—packed my bag, left the house, and moved in with my aunt that summer.

To pay for college, I worked full-time while I went to school full-time. What would've broken most college students my age only made me stronger. Although I have a wonderful relationship with my family now, that was a difficult time in my life, and I grew stronger and more fearless in the process. I went through many trials during those years—many ups and some downs; many good decisions and some poor ones. Since I basically had a crash course about life in general, I ended up feeling like there was nothing I couldn't do. I became fearless. I grew up privileged, but when I left home, I learned what it was like to live in poverty. Still, I held onto my middleclass ways and expectations. I didn't want to own a used car since I wouldn't have anyone to help me if something happened to it. Since that was the case, I had to work hard so I could buy a new car and afford everything else I needed during that difficult time in my life.

I remember having a job at a clothing store at the mall so I could readily purchase nice clothes at a discounted rate. I also worked at my favorite hot dog place back then, Nathan's, where I was permitted to eat for free during my shift. I even worked the midnight shift as a telephone dispatcher at a security firm to make extra money for tuition. During the summers, I'd work at a large bank or credit card call center. By the time my senior year in college rolled around, I had already worked for several well-known banks, and had my sights set on attending an Ivy League grad school and eventually becoming a college president. Despite my apparent limitations, I had become fearless.

In my younger years, before moving more specifically toward becoming a college president, I wanted to work on Wall Street—despite the fact that I had no real financial or banking experience. So, I did some research and learned that Goldman Sachs was the number one financial firm in the world at that time, so I wanted to be part of it.

Since I remember praying intensely about it, I shouldn't have been surprised by the call I received from a recruiter a few months later. Would I be interested in leaving Philadelphia once I graduated from the University of Pennsylvania to take a job at Goldman Sachs? I was stunned and jumped in with both feet. Soon after, the firm flew me into New York for an interview and I got the job. Once I was settled in, the hiring manager told me she'd decided to bring me on board because—although my background was so different—I had the skills and talents the company needed for the position, so they took a chance on me.

Then, September 11, 2001 happened. During that time, I lived in New Jersey and took the train into New York City, where the last stop was the World Trade Center. On that fateful day, I found myself in a position I never thought I'd be in: running for my life. My train had just arrived at Tower 2 when Tower 1 was hit by a plane piloted by terrorists.

The chaos was indescribable. I witnessed falling debris maiming people, watched people plummet to their deaths from the blazing fire above me, and saw children trampled by crowds running for safety.

As I made my way to our corporate headquarters, I stopped to help others impacted by the pandemonium—like the elderly couple whose bags had been toppled and the mother whose baby had been jostled out of her carriage. I guided them out of harm's way into a nearby bodega, then ran until I finally arrived at our building. I thought I was safe when I got to my office floor at the bank, but then learned we had lost many of our associates and friends who worked in the towers.

In the ensuing days after that tragic event, my reawakening began. As my spirit stirred, I began to see that I had a greater purpose and assignment on this earth and that God had spared me to achieve it. From that day forward, I felt indestructible. I knew God had me and that I was on a Kingdom assignment. I realized that of the seven spheres of influence, education and business were the two areas where I could make the most difference. From that day on, I never feared closed doors in academia, ministry, business, or entrepreneurial ventures. In this book, I touch on some of the challenging experiences I've faced at work along the way. I never ran from a problem; in fact, I tend to run *to* problems. More often than not, problems find me, and my ability to solve those problems has given me a reputation as a turnaround manager of sorts. Like young David, I never saw my size or my lack of knowledge or experience as a hindrance. Instead, with the help of the Holy Spirit, I fearlessly and boldly walked into my calling.

But this book isn't about me. It's about you. It's about God's greatness in you and the treasures He has bound up in your heart. In the age of COVID-19, we can submit to fear and allow it to determine our present and our future, or we can take the worst of circumstances and move forward with confidence—knowing that as long as we are hand-in-hand with the One who created the universe, we are sure to come out on top.

Reflection Points ~~~~~~~~~~~~~~~~~~~~~~~~~~~~~

Just like David, you have a choice every day. You can choose to fearlessly and boldly pursue your dreams, purposes, and calling—or you can shrink back and hope for the best.

As a leader, you will stand out when you have the courage to do what no one else will do and to step out or step up when no one else will. If you'll push back against fear and choose boldness with God instead, there's no limit to what you will be able to accomplish.

Remember, in the eyes of the world, David was not supposed to amount to much. He certainly wasn't supposed to ascend to the throne. But his fearless nature, dogged determination, and full reliance on the God of Israel lifted him to unimaginable heights.

~~~~~~

Into Action

The principle of this chapter is "Transcend Fear to Be Bold." Take a few minutes to write down specific ways you can apply this principle within your professional role or setting. The following questions can help you get started:

- Do you know what your dreams are as professional? Describe them.

- Do you have a strong sense of the purposes God has for your professional life? Write them down.

- Do you have a strong sense of the calling God has for you? Explain it as if talking to a friend.

If you weren't able to answer those questions easily, I encourage you to spend some focused time in prayer and Scripture, asking for God's help in guiding you.

Once you've clearly defined your dreams, purposes, and call for your professional life, determine what barriers may be holding you back from achieving them—which may include related anxieties and fears. Take a few minutes to write them down in the context of each question you answered previously.

Now, for the most important part: creating a plan to address the barriers you've just listed. You may be able to do this on your own, or you may want to ask a mentor or other trusted advisor for help. Either way, your plan should include both short-term and longer-term goals—as well as an outline of the specific steps needed to achieve them. Offer this process up to God and ask Him to help you create your plan and provide what's needed to see it through.

A Declaration of Boldness

While the wicked flee though no one pursues them, I am righteous and as bold as a lion. Wherever I go and whatever I do, I am strong and courageous. I will not be afraid nor will I panic because the Lord my God personally goes ahead of me; He will neither fail me nor abandon me. For I can do all things through Christ who gives me strength.

I am being made perfect in love, so every fear is being driven out of me and far from me. There is no fear in love, and since God is love, and I am in God, the spirit of fear has no hold on me. On the contrary, God has not given me a spirit of fear, but of power and of love and of a sound mind.

When I feel afraid, I will put my trust in the living God. I will praise Him for what He has promised. Since I trust in God, I don't need to be afraid of anything or anyone. With God on my side, who can harm me? When I seek the Lord, He will hear me and deliver me from all my fears.

Since I am filled with the Spirit of God, I am filled with courage and boldness to do what He has called me to do and be who He has called me to be. I will not shrink back in fear; I have extraordinary boldness and courage because I've been with Jesus.

Scripture References

Proverbs 28:1

Deuteronomy 31:6

Philippians 4:13

1 John 4:18

2 Timothy 1:7

Psalm 56:3-4

Psalm 34:4

Acts 4:13

2

WHEN YOU FAIL,
FAIL FORWARD

For a righteous man may fall seven times, and rise again…

Proverbs 24:16a (NKJV)

O f all the chapters in this book, this one was the most difficult for me to write—since I'll be discussing my experiences with failure in my personal life, at work, and spiritually. Three
areas of a person's life that are the most significant.

Honestly, I originally planned to place this chapter at the end of
the book, but I decided that what I'm trying to share here may
be better understood within the context of God's hand on my life
throughout my life—which has been especially powerful during
seasons of difficulty and perceived failures. In the following chapters, I'll be sharing about many of the things I've been blessed to
achieve as a professional and leader, and I want to establish early
on that I know none of that would have been possible without
God's never-ending help.

So, I'm going to couch those descriptions of success by first talking about failure—because we'll all experience it. But the good news is that failure in any form can provide some of the richest soil in which God can grow and nurture us for His purposes.

For a good part of my young adult life, I lived by the mantra that failure was not an option. But as I've gained more experience and matured, I've come to realize that failure is not only an option—it's an inevitability.

After all, despite my successes and the valuable learnings I've included in this book, I've had a considerable number of personal failures from failed exams, failing to meet my wellness and financial objectives, and most of all, failed relationships. I've failed many times in my life, but through it all, I chose—and I continue to choose—to fail forward. In fact, I rarely look back in my personal rearview mirror except to remind myself of what not to do.

Managing a multitude of relationships takes a great deal of time and is one of the most difficult things to master because you deal with individuals, their personalities, hurts, struggles, perceptions, and life-long experiences—all within day-to-day situations. While some people are easy enough to relate to, there are others you may wish were not placed in your path at all.

As many people do, I had a variety of deep hurts growing up that influenced my ability to relate to others in a healthy way. Since I was socially naïve as a young woman, I often found myself caught in a vicious cycle of being too trusting, getting hurt, and then not trusting at all. That carried over into my adult life, too.

From college to my thirties, while most things were going well in my life professionally, my romantic relationships and my marriage eventually failed. During this time, my experiences in these failed relationships could have been the storyline for an incredible novel, daytime soap opera, or reality show. I was lied to, cheated on, and emotionally hurt. Nonetheless, these experiences are key components of my testimony and have enabled me to minister to multitudes of women and men on the topic of marriage, divorce, and overall relationship challenges and triumphs.

Thankfully, there were good times, too—because even when I felt like I failed within these heartbreaking relationships, I got back up and tried again. I attempted to learn from my past mistakes, and each time, I hoped and prayed for a better outcome. I expected a better outcome. I hurt. I cried. I screamed. I laughed hysterically when there was nothing funny. I fell to my knees and on my face and prayed. I cried out to the Lord. I sought out a spiritual counselor. I read self-help books. I read Bible verses and chapters about relationships. I took care of myself. I loved and forgave myself. I asked God and others, whom I knowingly or unknowingly may have hurt, for forgiveness…and I let it all go. I did not wallow in my tears or dwell on my circumstances. I assessed my faults in the matter, got out of the situation quickly, and I moved forward.

As a result of these experiences, I allowed myself to become completely numb to relationships. I trusted no one. I was alone and grew to be quite comfortable with it. I always found solace in my work, so I spent most of my time at work or volunteering at church (which required dealing with lots of people but under different circumstances). In my supervisory capacity, I didn't believe in making friends at work—especially with peers or direct reports.

Over the years, I've found that accepting a leadership position can isolate you from others. My staff and those around me knew that I cared about them because every so often I came out of my shell and did something funny or thoughtful and unexpected for the team. I loved them and truly cared for them, but many of them never knew that because I kept my distance.

I often felt I was cheating myself and them out of sharing the love, fun, caring, and memorable times we could have had together as workmates because of my fear of intimacy in the workplace. Obviously, it makes sense for people to guard themselves and their actions in the office. You cannot befriend everyone, particularly when you're in a supervisory capacity. But where do you draw the line between being perceived as unsociable and detached rather than as a loving, kind, caring, Christ-like person?

Although no one ever told me this, I believe the reason some of my work relationships didn't reach their greatest potential was because I had relationship or trust issues. My husband really helped me understand that. He has an amazing ability to tell me all about myself (with some added exaggeration and personal speculation sprinkled in!). One thing he believes in very strongly is letting people feel your heart—especially those who work with you. You have to show them love in a personal way so they know that you care and that you love them. I agree with him, but I often worry about people taking advantage in that scenario, so, honestly, I'm still working on that.

I thought I was doing okay when people walked into my office to share their familial concerns or other troubles with me so I could pray for them. I thought I was showing them love and empathy, but really showing them love would have required asking how they were later, or placing a note in their mailbox and letting them know that I was praying for them. It might also have included cutting them some slack and showing grace when they were not meeting their work obligations or my expectations on the job.

I realize now that the things I didn't think to say or do on a regular basis that could have enriched my relationships may have resulted in missed opportunities to create something really positive. In my workplace scenarios, my failure was in not realizing that these individuals had been entrusted to me for care and nurturing, and to share the love of Christ. God had called me to impact people in a deeper way beyond my professional role.

Despite these perceptions of failure, I continued to move forward in making my relationships better each day with the Lord's help. Now, when I sense that I may have failed someone or the Lord in a connection that He wanted me to make, I commit to praying for that person. I also pray for myself, and I ask God to give me another chance to make things right.

Over the years, and by God's grace, I've experienced exponential spiritual growth. I've taught Sunday school, completed ministry school, preached, participated in mission work abroad, read the Bible from cover to cover several times, fasted and prayed, helped the needy, sick, orphans and widows, paid my tithes, spread the Gospel, and led people to salvation. Through His grace and mercy, I attempt to live a godly life, and I consistently work toward being a virtuous woman. When my assignment on this earth has been completed, I want to hear God say, "Well done, good and faithful servant!" (Matthew 25:21, NIV).

But in many ways, I still fail to be consistent in these areas. I fail at meditating on the Word of God consistently. As a busy professional, it can be easy to find excuses for not spending adequate—or in some cases, any—time on a given day with the Lord. I find myself so busy that I'm unable to spend a quiet moment to listen to the promptings of the Holy Spirit or to journal my thoughts or directions from God.

And I sometimes fail at loving my neighbor as I should. I don't make enough time to love on people and to open their minds to what it means to be a follower of Jesus Christ. I could be a better wife, sister, daughter, friend, coworker, and church member.

As I write these words, if I were to grade myself, I'd get a "B" based on where I feel I want and need to be spiritually on a consistent basis. We must all be willing to critically and truthfully examine ourselves and assess if we need a spiritual boost to reconnect with Christ, Who is our lifeline and the Vine from which all good things are produced (John 15:1-8). We are nothing without the Body of Christ and we would surely be spiritually dead without the Word of God.

In academia, if a student takes an exam and doesn't have the content memorized in order to apply it or the proper nourishment to sustain them during the exam, they'll likely fail the test. This applies to our spiritual life, too. We must spend time with the Lord, eat His Word, and produce fruit on our branches as a result of being connected to the Vine. Only then will others be able to benefit from our fruit and recognize the need for this same type of connection so they can bear fruit of their own.

The nature of our humanity and sin means that even as Christians, we'll likely fail in some way on a regular basis. However, when this happens, God wants us to ask for His forgiveness and then pick up our mats and move forward within His grace (John 5:8).

In fact, failure is a topic that's covered a lot in the Bible; from its opening verses to its final pages, God's Word is replete with stories of men and women who made choices that led to failure. Failure is a part of life, and it's an important part of the human experience because it's how we grow, mature, and learn. That's why accounts of failure in the Bible make me feel better, since they remind me that I'm not the only one who makes mistakes.

But the most amazing thing of all is this: even though people in the Bible failed, that's not where their story ended; often they were restored, redeemed, and used by God in spite of their failures.

That was the case with Paul, Barnabas, and Barnabas' cousin, John Mark (or Mark, who wrote the gospel of Mark). The relationship between these men became complicated. Paul and Barnabas had enjoyed a close relationship ever since Barnabas spoke up for Paul (former Christian-persecuting Saul) and insisted that the believers accept him as a newly-transformed brother in Christ (Acts 9:26-27).

Then, one day when the church was praying, the Holy Spirit indicated that Paul and Barnabas had a special work to do and Mark accompanied them to the island of Cyprus as their "assistant." After Paul ministered to the governor, they sailed on to Pamphylia. Then the Bible says, "There John Mark left them and returned to Jerusalem" (Acts 13:1-14, NLT).

The Bible doesn't give specifics as to why Mark turned back and went home; some scholars think Mark didn't agree with spreading the gospel to the Gentile world while others say he may have been afraid of the physical dangers they would encounter on the trip. But one thing is very clear: Paul was extremely upset that Mark had left them in the middle of their ministry assignment. Unfortunately, this caused a rift between Paul and Barnabas:

"After some time Paul said to Barnabas, 'Let's go back and visit each city where we previously preached the word of the Lord, to see how the new believers are doing.' Barnabas agreed and wanted to take along John Mark. But Paul disagreed strongly, since John Mark had deserted them in Pamphylia and had not continued with them in their work. Their disagreement was so sharp that they separated. Barnabas took John Mark with him and sailed for Cyprus. Paul chose Silas, and as he left, the believers entrusted him to the Lord's gracious care" (Acts 15:36-40, NLT).

We really can't blame Paul here, can we? Mark abandoned them the last time they took him on a ministry trip, and Paul didn't want it to happen again. Mark had broken Paul's trust, and even though Barnabas seemed to forgive and forget, Paul wasn't ready to do the same. It appears that Barnabas and Mark had a chance to reconcile their relationship, so Barnabas was ready to include Mark in the work of the ministry again. But the relationship between Paul and Mark was still strained, and Paul was unwilling to allow Mark to accompany them on the next ministry trip.

Barnabas was so furious that Paul wouldn't allow Mark to come with them that Barnabas refused to travel with Paul! The men split up; Barnabas took Mark to Cyprus, and Paul selected Silas to accompany him. Apparently, this was a pretty big disagreement for the men to completely part ways, but the Bible doesn't give us any specifics about it.

Likewise, the Bible doesn't give us details about Paul and Mark reconciling, but it appears they did. While Paul was in prison, he wrote in 2 Timothy 4:11, "Only Luke is with me. Bring Mark with you when you come, for he will be helpful to me in my ministry" (NLT). This verse seems to indicate that John Mark overcame his failure, was redeemed, and became a great support and comforter for Paul while he was in prison.

Later, in Philemon 1:24, Paul calls Mark his "coworker." And in Colossians 4:10, Paul writes to the church in Colossae, "Aristarchus, who is in prison with me, sends you his greetings, and so does Mark, Barnabas' cousin. As you were instructed before, make Mark welcome if he comes your way." No longer seeing Mark as a deserter but as a faithful and reliable ministry partner, Paul instructs the church to welcome Mark.

This says a lot about Mark. Rather than letting his early failure disqualify him from future ministry and success, he worked to reconcile himself to those he let down, and he grew in maturity, faithfulness, and leadership. It's likely that in order for Paul and Mark's relationship to be restored, there had to be repentance and forgiveness on both sides. Then Mark likely had to prove himself—he had to put action to his words—by showing that he wouldn't fail or falter in the work of the ministry again.

We can learn a couple of valuable lessons from Mark.

> First, we must acknowledge that failure
> happens and what you do with failure is what
> matters most.

Everyone fails; if it's you, then fail forward. Own up to it, and do what you can to fix the situation or relationship. If it's someone else, demonstrate grace and allow the person to be reconciled and to be part of the solution.

Second, we must learn to be patient with ourselves and others. Remember how God treats you when you fail Him, and do the same for others and yourself.

I will leave you with a quote from best-selling author Denis Waitley, who I believe captures the essence of failing forward and reminds us that every setback is a setup for greater things:

"Failure should be our teacher, not our undertaker. Failure is delay, not defeat. It is a temporary detour, not a dead end. Failure is something we can avoid only by saying nothing, doing nothing, and being nothing."

May the God who has redeemed failure time and time again and turned it around for His glory continue to bless you, keep you, and prosper you until the glorious day when He returns to claim His own. Amen.

Reflection Points

Failure, for lack of a better word, is yucky. It's yucky to think about, yucky to talk about, and certainly—from this writer's perspective—yucky to write about. Even if we try to shield ourselves from it by ignoring it or not focusing on it, failure is inevitable. However, if failure is embraced rather than eschewed, it can often lead to greater success. Actually, there are many examples of failures-turned-successes across the business world because those behind them failed to give up.

Into Action

The principle of this chapter is "When You Fail, Fail Forward," which implies the fact that we shouldn't allow our inevitable failures to define us or hold us back from all that God wants to achieve in our lives. As we discussed in this chapter, God can turn our failures into some of our greatest gifts, if we can embrace His forgiveness, strength, and redemption within that process.

So, how about you? On both a personal and professional level, what failures from your past are you falsely believing God cannot redeem? Take a few minutes and write them down.

Now, do a topical search for scripture passages about failure. You can do that through an online search or through use of a topical reference. I bet you'll be surprised at the long list of passages that will appear! Next, pick at least five references to dig into further. Once you've read through them, take the time needed to journal about the passage. Include your thoughts about the impact of failure on the person involved and how God used that situation to transform the perceived negatives of failure into something positive.

Next, apply what you learned within this activity to your own life. Where have you failed in the past and experienced God's transformative power? What failures do you presently perceive in your personal or professional life that you're hanging onto instead of turning them over to your Redeemer, Who loves you so?

Once you've identified perceived failures that continue to hold you back, ask God for His help in addressing them as appropriate. You may want to ask a trusted friend or faith leader to provide a little support.

As you journey through this process, you'll be better able to be bold in embracing failure as a pathway to success. By the power of the Holy Spirit, turn fear into strength. Trust that the One who gave you a vision will be faithful to see it completed and will work out details and circumstances you don't presently understand.

The "failure" you believe you're experiencing is an opportunity to submit fully to God and to seek His solutions instead of your own. Today, will you take the first step toward Him to do that?

A Prayer of Strength

When I fail, I will remember that though the righteous fall seven times, they rise again, but the wicked stumble when calamity strikes. Thank You, God, that You help me when I'm in trouble; You lift me when I call. I won't be afraid, for You are with me; I won't be dismayed, for You are my God. You will strengthen me and help me; You will uphold me with Your righteous right hand.

Since all have sinned and fall short of the glory of God, I realize that failure has been a part of my life, and I will continue to fail sometimes. Help me to have Your perspective on my failures, Lord; when I am afflicted and troubled, remind me that I have the opportunity to learn Your statutes and lean on Your strength and wisdom in the midst of my failure.

I will remember that even though I feel hard pressed on every side, I am not crushed; sometimes I feel perplexed, but I'm not in despair; when I feel persecuted, I am not abandoned; when I'm struck down, I am not destroyed. I will press on with God's grace and strength, forgetting the things that are behind and reaching out for the things that are ahead, striving toward the prize of the upward call of God in Christ Jesus. I will trust the Lord with all my heart and not depend on my own understanding. As I remember the Lord in all I do, He will give me extravagant success.

Glory to God. Hallelujah! Amen.

Scripture References

Proverbs 24:16

Psalm 145:14

Isaiah 41:10

Romans 3:23

Psalm 119:71

Philippians 3:13-14

2 Corinthians 4:8-9

Proverbs 3:5-6

3

WALK IN YOUR
GOD-GIVEN PURPOSE,
NOT THE WORLD'S

*Many are the plans in a person's heart, but it is the LORD's purpose
that prevails.*

Proverbs 19:21 (NIV)

In a day and age where money is scarce and stretching a dollar essential, many are more intentional about pursuing possibilities that will financially benefit them. But when money and success are pursued for the wrong reasons, sin can more easily find an opening to dig its talons into both our pocketbooks and our souls. Unfortunately, even God's children aren't immune to this harmful dynamic.

In reality, everyone is vulnerable to the discontent that's fueled by a desire for more—and the materialistic society we live in feeds this craving continually. Social media, superfluous television commercials, and provocative magazine covers beckon to us constantly: Drive this fancy car; live in this beautiful home; own this perfect body. In the process of being lured into such fantasies, it can be easy to ignore the costs that may be associated with pursuing them. The fact that many are willing to spend without limit to achieve their heart's desire or the social status they crave is a sad reflection of the emptiness that too many feel.

Even more troublesome is the impact these dynamics can have on how Christians use their funds. Those who fail to tithe because they fear there won't be enough money to support the lifestyles they've become accustomed to display disobedience to God's priorities and risk the loss of blessings He promises to provide. In this context, the very people who should know better may be among those who are most often deceived.

In our current times, too many want everything and they want it now. Some even believe they are entitled to having whatever they want when they want it, and are "owed" that which others work so hard to achieve. Such achievers finish their education and participate in the workforce; embrace entrepreneurship and start their own business; or go to college and earn a degree to practice a profession they'll enjoy. Upstanding citizens like these aren't looking for easy, passive, and sometimes unethical or illegal paths to achieving their dreams—instead, they're getting there by doing the hard work that's required.

But even when this is the case, leaving God out of the equation still leads to less-than-optimal results. Even those who pursue their dreams with integrity and eventually reach what they set out to do will come up empty on the inside if they fail to prioritize God's purposes along the way. That's why there are scores of people today who are so dissatisfied with their lives and their choice of profession. Even those who are quite successful may wake up in the morning with a deep sense of unfulfillment.

I remember reading a true story about an American businessman who was living a very lavish life as a stockbroker. But during the last U.S. recession, he lost it all—the money, the cars, and the real estate. One day he decided to set his house on fire while he was still in it. He killed himself because he had lost all of his worldly possessions. Apparently, this man believed his life no longer had purpose.

As Christians, we are assured that we do have a purpose here on this earth. God created us to be in relationship with Him and to accomplish His purposes for our lives in His perfect timing—but we have to be active participants in that process. It's only when we're walking in our God-defined purpose that we can begin to see the abundance, blessings, and prosperity that He has in store for us.

So, if you're chasing money, stop. Instead, chase your purpose with God.

During my formative years, my parents urged me to become a doctor or engineer. They considered these to be worthwhile careers that would yield an abundance of income. But, I chose another route and became an administrator in the field of education. I knew I'd never make millions in this profession, but that didn't matter to me. From an early age, God gave me clarity about my purpose. Administrating was something I was particularly skilled at doing, and it was something I was very passionate about. When you have both skill and passion related to something, that can be a clear indication of the specific gifts God has given you and the purpose He has for you.

Though I've been working in higher education for most of my professional life, I also worked in the banking industry when I was just getting started. In my early 20's while working in a particularly lucrative position in which I out-earned all my peers, I was accustomed to limos driving me home; my dinners being paid for; and living in the vibrant environment of downtown New York City. In my ignorance, I believed I was living the life, but I often felt empty inside. Most of the time I was satisfied, but there was little joy in my heart.

Have you ever felt that way? Have you ever felt like you should be happy because things are going really well for you—you're making great money, you have recognition in your job, you've been promoted—and yet there's still an emptiness inside of you? From my experience I can tell you that emptiness is there because you're not walking in your purpose. And as long as you continue to walk outside of your purpose, you will experience those feelings of emptiness and confusion, and in some cases, despair.

September 11, 2001 changed things for a lot people—including me. Surviving the World Trade Center attacks really put things into perspective for me. I realized that for me to be happy, productive, and effective in my life, I needed to leave the financial world and return to higher education because it's what I was called to do. I've been happy ever since I made that decision; in fact, other opportunities have opened up to me as a result, and I've been able to fulfill another part of my calling: to establish The Global Christian Professional Women's Association (GCPWA).

Through this organization, I build up professionals in Christ; undertake entrepreneurial ventures and philanthropic activities that empower people; and accept frequent speaking engagements that change people's lives and help mobilize them. These ventures bring me great satisfaction and have allowed me to bless and positively affect the lives of many people. I'm convinced that we shouldn't want to leave this world the way we found it;

> We should operate in our God-given purpose
> and leave this world better than we found it,
> just like Jesus did.

As I drew closer to God in my new season of life, I began to realize that I was in fact walking in my purpose. Blessings were poured out on me because of my obedience to my calling and because I was walking in the will of God. The high salary of my early years has carried over to a field which isn't known for its lucrative pay. However, I believe I've been blessed in this way because God gifted me to do the work I'm doing—which helps me to do it with passion and excellence. As I've walked in my purpose, God has rewarded me for doing so.

In this life, there are times when we must reject what our minds, the people around us, and societal norms are telling us to do. Instead, we must tap into what God has for us—which is even greater than all we can ever ask or think (Ephesians 3:20).

My husband, James, is a prime example of this principle. As a young man, he started out in the military where he pursued academic degrees in criminal justice and political science. He graduated from college and started a career in law enforcement, then went on to law school, since he was passionate about advocating for others. However, he wasn't happy pursuing the law degree and working in that field even though it provided financial security for him (something he didn't have growing up as the youngest of seven children in a very impoverished and rural area of the country).

As a child, James was an outstanding singer and was musically inclined, even playing the piano and trumpet naturally. James loves people, and he enjoys making them laugh. One day, while he was enrolled in graduate school, there was a talent competition for comedians, so he decided to try his hand and easily won. In fact, he was so gifted in this area that he won every single competition he entered after that. It quickly became clear that this was his calling—to bring joy to others through laughter and entertainment.

Once he accepted his calling, he worked hard at it (faith without works is dead) which led him to grander stages—including every major television network. James is not a planner, but God had a plan for his life. So he just followed his heart and his passion, trusting God to take care of the rest.

As a result, James has performed for three U.S. presidents. For many years, he was one of the few comedians who was approved to perform for Ronald McDonald House Charities. He has performed for numerous high-level corporations, opened up for Aretha Franklin at Carnegie Hall, toured with Ray Charles and Garth Brooks, and even been on a TV show with Jennifer Aniston and Wayne Knight.

While James is one of the few comedic actors and impressionists still working full-time in his profession today, he could have been an even bigger deal—if he had chased the money. Many of his friends are celebrity household names, and James could have followed the same path. Instead, he continued to develop his relationship with the Lord over the years; this kept him sane and grounded at the height of his career when he worked in worldly places, like Los Angeles.

James chased God, not money. That's why he wakes up every day feeling joyful about the fact that he's fulfilling God's purpose for his life. He's honored that there are people who come to see his shows from all over the world, and through their laughter, many have been miraculously healed. God is working through James' gift to change people's lives—which is what it looks like to chase one's purpose instead of money and material success.

When Jesus walked this earth, He called many people to join His cause and help Him fulfill His purpose: preaching the Kingdom of God, healing the sick, and freeing those in spiritual bondage. Early in His ministry, Jesus chose twelve men to be His disciples. Matthew (a despised tax collector) and John (a fisherman) were among Jesus' original disciples. Luke (a physician) and Mark (or John Mark, an evangelist) joined Matthew and John in writing accounts of the life of Jesus after careful research and from personal experience.

These four men are worth studying because they were prominent figures in Jesus' ministry—and because they chased Jesus instead of money or success.

Mark is credited with writing the earliest account of Jesus' life and ministry. While it›s the shortest of the Gospels, it's action-packed. Even though Mark wasn't one of Jesus' 12 disciples, he and his family were clearly followers of Jesus. Mark's mother regularly held prayer meetings in her home and his family must have been wealthy, since they often entertained guests and had a servant girl who answered the door (Acts 12:11-13). But Mark didn't simply ride on the family's coattails and enjoy the family fortune; instead, he traveled with the Apostle Paul, Barnabas, and the Apostle Peter to spread the good news of Jesus Christ. He chased after God's Kingdom, not money or worldly success.

Luke, on the other hand, wrote the longest of the four Gospels— as well as the book of Acts. In fact, he was the only non-Jew to write part of the New Testament. Luke was an associate of Paul and traveled with him on several of his missionary journeys. As we would expect of a doctor, Luke's account of the life of Jesus is full of healing stories. Luke was well-educated and observant and could have made lots of money working in the health field of his day, but he chose to chase after the Great Physician and fulfill his purpose—to write a detailed account of the Messiah's life and ministry for billions of people to read.

Matthew wrote an account of Jesus' ministry in Hebrew. As a tax collector, he knew how to read and write, so he had very valuable skills for that time. Most tax collectors were dishonest and charged people much more than needed, pocketing the rest for themselves. As a result, the community hated them, but they had plenty of money. However, in Matthew's case, instead of dishonestly raking in the cash, Matthew responded to the call of the Messiah; he became one of Jesus' twelve disciples and participated in spreading the good news of the Kingdom of God.

Referred to as the "beloved disciple," John was also one of the twelve disciples and enjoyed the most intimate friendship with Jesus. His family owned a fishing business with employees, so they likely weren't hurting for money (Mark 1:20). All John would've had to do was continue working in the family business, and he would've been all set. However, when the Messiah called him, he left his father in the boat "without delay" and followed his new Lord. That one decision changed the course of his life forever—and ours—since he also penned an account of the life and ministry of Jesus.

What do all these men have in common?

Each stepped away from their business or profession to pursue Christ. They all had success at their fingertips, but they would've totally missed their purposes if they had rejected Jesus' call and instead chased worldly success.

Imagine where we would be today had these men not put their "normal lives" on hold and recorded what they saw and heard Jesus say and do. What if they had rejected Jesus' call? Would someone else have written down such details about the life of Christ? Of course, God would have achieved His purposes either way—but these men would have missed out on the opportunity of a lifetime if they'd chosen differently.

There's a final point about what all these men share: they each embody the teaching of Matthew 6:33 by the way they lived their lives: "But seek first his kingdom and his righteousness, and all these things will be given to you as well" (NIV).

This is a promise we can build our lives on, too. God isn't against us having success—but He doesn't want us to let the pursuit of it get in the way of focusing on His purpose and plan for our lives, since that will have such a detrimental effect. Instead, He wants us to seek Him and His Kingdom first, so He can then provide the abundance He wants to pour into our lives.

As my husband has discovered, when our relationship with Jesus is our top priority, we'll then be able to embrace God's specific purposes and subsequently enjoy the success, peace, joy and fulfillment only He can provide.

So, like the writers of the Gospels, don't chase money and success. Chase your purpose in Christ—and all these blessings will be given to you as well.

Reflection Points

When we hear the stories of how Jesus called His disciples, we tend to gloss over a very crucial part of the narrative: The immediacy with which they made their decisions to follow Him. When Jesus called His first two disciples, Simon and Andrew, we are told they followed Him "at once" (Mark 1:18, NIV). When He called Matthew, the tax collector "got up and followed Him" (Mark 2:14, NIV). There was something about Jesus that signaled immediacy and urgency to those He called. I believe that "something" was the way He communicated His divine mission and purpose.

News flash – people love vision! They are drawn to it like moths to a light. When we come face-to-face with someone who knows exactly what they're doing, where they're going, and how they're going to get there, we are magnetically drawn to them. This is the reason many leaders have made indelible marks on this world and why people have left everything to follow them.

Success is fleeting. Fame and riches are temporal. And purpose and passion can't be bought. Instead, they are divine endowments. When individuals discover their God-given gifts and align them with God's mission for their lives, a congruency is created that far outweighs all the riches of this world.

Here's truth: God called you. Yes, you.

He placed unique gifts and talents into you for the furtherance of His kingdom. If you have never explored those gifts and if you are still uncertain as to why you are here, I implore you to devote yourself to digging into this area of your life.

~~~~~~

Into Action

The principle of this chapter is "Walk in Your God-Given Purpose, Not the World's." Do you know what God's purpose is for you? Throughout all your days, He has been giving you clues about it. The things you love, that drive you crazy, and that you're passionate about—they're all clues about your greater Kingdom purpose.

By now, you know there's an assignment coming—and here it is: Go on a scavenger hunt with God. That's right, take some time to examine the clues He has been placing in your life regarding the purpose(s) He has for you. Here are a few prompts to get you started:

- Name the top five things you love or love to do.

- Name the top five things that drive you crazy.

- Name the top five things you're passionate about.

Of course, just because something tops the list in one of those categories doesn't mean it's part of God's plans for you. So, the next step is to spend time praying and journaling about whether the things you listed are pleasing to Him and play a role in His purposes for you. Be sure to have your Bible handy to see what Scripture says about it, too. God has already provided a single, authoritative volume of clear guidance about all kinds of topics there—if we'll only take the time needed to explore what He says.

Once you've defined God's purposes for you, the next question relates to your level of commitment to fulfilling them. In this reflection, we've examined the immediacy with which Jesus' disciples dropped everything to follow Him. As you draw nearer to God and He reveals these things to you, will you be willing to do the same?

A Prayer of Purpose and Contentment

Lord, I will not be like unbelievers who run after riches and material things, for You know what I need, Heavenly Father. Instead, I will seek first Your Kingdom and Your righteousness, and You will give me all these things as well. No matter what it costs me personally or professionally, I will let my light shine before others so they may see my good deeds and glorify my Father in heaven. I will not be afraid or ashamed to go into all the world and preach the gospel to every creature.

While I have many plans in my heart, may Your purpose for my life prevail. I know that You have plans for me — plans for good and not for disaster, to give me a future and a hope. I know that for everything there's a season, so I will trust Your timing and exercise patience. There's a time for every purpose under heaven, so I will trust that all things are working together for my good because I love You and I'm called according to Your purpose.

Father, I realize that You will reward me according to my conduct and as my deeds deserve, so help me to honor You wherever I am employed and in whatever position I serve. In the end, more than anything, I want to hear You say, "Well done, good and faithful servant! You have been faithful with a few things; I will put you in charge of many things. Come and share your master's happiness!"

Hallelujah! Amen.

Scripture References

Matthew 6:32-33

Matthew 5:16

Mark 16:15

Proverbs 19:21

Jeremiah 29:11

Ecclesiastes 3:1

Romans 8:28

Jeremiah 32:19

Matthew 25:21

4

OWN YOUR POSITION, WITH GOD'S HELP

Then David fled from Naioth at Ramah and went to Jonathan and asked, "What have I done? What is my crime? How have I wronged your father, that he is trying to take my life?"

I Samuel 20:1 (NIV)

David couldn't figure it out. He had worked diligently under the king's careful tutelage and thought he had earned his unconditional trust. In fact, he had proven himself so capable that the king had given him carte blanche to run the day-to-day operations of the nation's military. As a four-star general, he'd rightfully earned and demanded the utmost respect from his staff, the soldiers he led, and the subjects of the kingdom. His favorability ratings were sky high and his past scandal free. Even his enemies knew of his sterling reputation and respected him.

Yet, in the midst of David's unquestionable competence, the king grew suddenly resistant. Without warning, hostility and rejection emerged, which eventually led to sabotage. The king's jealousy-fueled cruelty even left David standing at the altar after the king promised his daughter's hand in marriage and then reneged at the eleventh hour.

Once David saw the proverbial writing on the wall, he fled the king's presence, emotionally wounded and confused. Undeterred, the king pursued David endlessly, determined to find him and destroy his reputation, his legacy, and end his life.

But why?

While I would never put myself on par with David and his storied accomplishments, this timeless story resonates deeply with me. I can empathize with this competent, faith-filled man who was unfairly marginalized by his superior.

Like David, I learned that neither my past accomplishments nor the depth of my bitterness would win the day. Instead, I found that I'd need to rise to a new level and kick into a higher gear I didn't even know I had.

I'm blessed to have worked at a number of high-ranking universities and institutions throughout my career. Through God's grace, I'd managed to build a reputation over the years as a turn-around manager who could get things done. So, when I was recruited to help my new employer address a difficult issue, I looked forward to the challenges ahead.

The supervisor I was assigned to had impeccable credentials and had made history at the institution by becoming the first African-American to head his prestigious department. As I stepped into the role, I expected to do well given my experience and looked forward to enjoying an additional edge due to commonalities with my new boss.

I quickly discovered that neither would be the case.

The dawning reality of my situation emerged within the first few weeks of starting my position. Through a series of events and conversations, I began to feel that I wasn't measuring up. What was even more painful was that my revered supervisor was the person who was particularly hard on me. He regularly redlined my work and questioned my actions. It was as if he felt I wasn't capable of meeting the expectations of my role. The seemingly needless and frequent criticisms chipped away at my defenses, eroded my confidence, and left me feeling frustrated and discouraged.

Before long, I found myself taking everything personally.

Why would you treat me like this?

I should be a trusted and treasured protégée to you.

Instead, I feel more certain each day that you don't want me to succeed in this role.

But why would that be?

In all my years of working in challenging environments as a leader, I'd never experienced anything like this. I had always exuded a high level of confidence and competence in all I had done. I had always met—and exceeded—every professional expectation I faced.

But now, for the first time in my career, I was apparently coming up short.

Each time I met with my supervisor, I felt more defeated and deflated. I began to allow self-pity and doubt to settle in. Eventually, I reasoned that I was past the point of no return and that it wasn't going to be possible to be successful in this job. I started to plan for my exit with a determination to leave on my terms, since being fired wasn't an acceptable option.

But God had other ideas.

One day, I felt a prompting by the Holy Spirit to take definitive action and do something about the situation rather than complain about what was happening to me. I made a new resolution to give 300 percent of myself to the job while relying and trusting entirely on the Lord. I pressed in on my prayers and believed wholeheartedly that I would emerge victorious. The Spirit directed me to study my boss closely in an effort to truly understand him. As author and Wharton management professor Michael Useem says, I planned to "lead up."

I began by examining the way he conducted himself in meetings. I asked myself what made him tick—which is when I started to realize he was a man with a stellar reputation to maintain. He was an incredibly astute individual who had excelled in all aspects of his career. His leadership acuity had propelled him to a prestigious role at one of the nation's most respected institutions. He was all about the business, and peak performance was the language he understood best. He wanted the work done and he wanted it done well.

Once I had a better understanding of the man I reported to, I started to up my game. I found myself anticipating his needs and started assuming greater responsibility for myself, my actions, and my work. Knowing that excellence honors both God and the people we work for, I embraced a new commitment to apply it to everything I did. I went the extra mile and attended to the most minute details. With God's help, I worked harder, longer, and more strategically. Since this was the most challenging position I'd ever held, I felt myself being propelled to a level of performance that exceeded what I'd delivered in the past.

The hard work paid off. By the grace of God, I was able to lead our department to a resolution of the difficulties I'd been hired to address. Once that immense task was behind us, I began to notice a change in my supervisor's demeanor and how he treated me. He seemed to have a newfound respect for me, and became more open and helpful. His criticisms waned and his compliments became more frequent—even about little things. It was a complete shift from what I'd been experiencing.

This dynamic evolved into a cherished relationship in which he became a true mentor for me and one of my greatest supporters. As a result, I was given continued opportunities that eventually propelled me into my dream job of being a college president. What a turn of events had occurred since the early days of our prickly relationship—in which this man had transformed from being my nemesis to becoming someone I could always count on for support.

But why?

Because the Holy Spirit directed me to *own* that first position in which I struggled. As a result, I worked hard and in the manner I knew was expected of me. I never figured out whether it was God who was testing me with the problems I was having with my supervisor or whether it was the Enemy who was attempting to block my success. Whatever it was, I believe I passed the test.

No matter what kind of supervisor you have—whether you like each other or not—you must remember that you have one common goal: to achieve the organization's objectives. If you can find a way to focus on that, you can usually win your supervisor's support.

Instead of taking things personally, try to remember this essential concept:

> The dynamics between you and your supervisor aren't about building a friendship or stroking your ego—but about getting the job done with excellence.

To help you do that, identify exactly what you need to do your job well by studying your supervisor and leading up. Try to gain a better understanding regarding his/her expectations for both you and the outcomes of your work. Remember that although some supervisors do serve as mentors, this is not always the case.

Of course, none of this is possible without prayer, praise, and faith. That's why you must prioritize your relationship with God so He can help you deal in a godly manner with whatever may come your way. Be constantly in prayer, so the Lord can enlighten you about how to handle difficult situations. Thank and praise Him for allowing you to be in a situation which can be used for His good and perfect purposes.

Remember, whatever you're going through at any given moment with your employer, God's got your back. He has a plan for your life that will work out for your benefit as you trust in Him—even if you can't see it just yet. He did it for me and He can certainly do it for you.

Reflection Points

In I Samuel 18-26, we read how David tried to do everything possible to win Saul's affection, adoration, and respect—but the opposite actually occurred. Instead of supporting David, he became jealous and envious to such an extreme he wanted to kill him. He became fearful of David's strength, charisma, competence, and success. Saul started believing that God loved David more than He loved him, and his insecurity led to his eventual downfall.

David ascended to his destiny because of God's ordination and because the cream always rises to the top. David was truly a leader. Everywhere he went—even in the caves while in exile—people followed him and pledged their allegiance to him. David conquered his foe because he trusted in God, studied his enemy, outsmarted him, and eventually was promoted to become king.

When faced with a situation that seems untenable with a supervisor or a superior, we can quickly forget who God made us to be. We can dismiss His manifold promises through the centuries and disregard the countless stories of the heroes of the faith—regular people who overcame insurmountable odds by remaining faithful to the end because they knew the Hand they clung to would not let them go.

~~~~~~

Into Action

The principle of this chapter is "Own Your Position, with God's Help." If you have leadership potential and apply it in the manner God desires, you will rise to the top, no matter where you are planted. However, if you give in to fears and insecurities when faced with workplace challenges, that will be more difficult to do. When we have a track record of professional success, we can be especially vulnerable to this dynamic when faced with challenges we didn't expect in new settings—which is why we must always remain sensitive to the need to assess each challenge with a fresh perspective.

In this chapter, I described the change that occurred when I asked for God's help in *owning* my position—i.e. taking responsibility for my own success instead of blaming my supervisor for what didn't seem to be working. If anything in this chapter sounds familiar to you, perhaps you need to do the same. Consider the following questions to determine if that may be the case:

- Did you agree with your supervisor's assessment of your performance on your last evaluation?

- Do you find yourself blaming your supervisor for things you view as out of your control?

- Do you find that feedback from your supervisor frequently hurts your feelings?

- When feedback is critical or negative in some way, do you find yourself taking it personally?

- Do you feel like it's no use, that your supervisor just doesn't "like" you?

If you answered "yes" to any of those questions, I encourage you to take your situation to God and ask for His help. The Bible is clear that God wants us to work with excellence in every instance, as if working for Him (Colossians 3:23)—and that's no different for your context of work.

Additionally, I described how I applied the concept of "leading up" to my difficult situation, which is a concept developed by author and Wharton management professor, Michael Useem. If you are not familiar with his work, or this concept, I encourage you to conduct further research to learn more about this approach and consider how it may apply to your situation.

But most of all, remember that God will do mighty things through those who seek Him first and honor Him in all they do. So, as you appropriately address your situation in the context described here— remember to cling to God and trust Him to take care of your needs.

A Prayer of Submission

Father, I feel overwhelmed whenever I think about my relationship with my supervisor. Thank You for being a generous God and promising to give me wisdom if I would only ask and not doubt. I desperately need Your supernatural wisdom about how to relate with and respect my supervisor. Therefore, I will walk in grace and respond with a gentle answer even when my supervisor treats me with anger or harshness.

I will do all things without murmuring or complaining; instead, I will have the same attitude as Christ Jesus: total humility. I confess that every word I speak and everything I do is characterized by genuine humility, authentic honor, and pure love. I refuse to pay back evil for evil, rather I always try to do good to everyone—even those who attack and harass me without reason. I choose to be submissive to my superior with all respect, even when he/she is being unreasonable or difficult.

Most days, I feel weary and weak from dealing with this stressful situation, but Your strength and power sustain me. And even though I face many trials and troubles, You rescue me every time. I will wait patiently for You, Lord; I know You hear my cry. You will bring me up out of this horrible pit, out of the miry clay, and set my feet upon a rock. You will establish my steps for Your glory. May my actions and words help my supervisor to see Your goodness and cause him/her to want to know You too.

In Jesus's name, amen.

Scripture References

James 1:5-6

Proverbs 15:1

Philippians 2:14

Philippians 2:5

1 Thessalonians 5:15

1 Peter 2:18-20

Isaiah 40:29

Psalm 34:19

Psalm 40:1-2

5

PRAY FOR THOSE
WHO PERSECUTE YOU

*A false witness shall not be unpunished, and he that speaketh lies
shall not escape.*

Proverbs 19:5 (KJV)

If nothing else, we could certainly characterize Haman as an "ambitious" man. More truthfully, words like "calculating," "ruthless," and "cunning," are probably closer to the mark. Endowed with a lofty position in the Persian government, Haman answered to no one but King Xerxes, who gave him a wide scope of authority and very little oversight. So immense was Haman's influence that all the king's officials would actually bow down before him in the ultimate act of reverence every time he walked by.

Well, that is, all except Mordecai.

Mordecai had earned a position in the government as one of the palace officials, which was quite advantageous because his cousin, Esther, was the newly-minted queen. Though their relationship was kept secret, his sage advice to her would quite often influence the king on matters of policy. Certain their presence at the palace was divinely ordained and for reasons far more grand than what they appeared, Mordecai was content to quietly lead from the shadows.

However, Haman wasn't nearly as content. The fact that all the palace officials bowed in his presence except Mordecai didn't sit well with him. After doing some digging, Haman discovered this rebel wasn't even Persian, he was a Jew! This new information stoked the fires of his scorn and lured him into an abyss of hatred—which was directed toward both his adversary and his adversary's entire race. Filled with rage, Haman didn't want to simply extinguish Mordecai; he wanted to wipe his people off the planet, too.

But there was a problem with his plan: it was way above his pay grade.

Since Haman couldn't act on his own, he approached the king and told him of a group of obstinate people who were trouble-makers and rabble-rousers and whose customs were in opposition to those of the Persians. For this reason, he argued, they should all be destroyed—and with the king's approval, Haman said he would gladly do the deed. In fact, so passionate was Haman about this project that he told the king there would be no need for the use of government funds. Instead, he'd be happy to finance the entire thing from his personal coffers.

And so it was.

With newly acquired powers of granting life and death in his hand, Haman left the palace that day feeling emboldened and proud. His first item of business was to order the construction of a 75-foot gallows to hang Mordecai. Indeed, if a mass extermination was about to occur, it would have to start with someone. Who better than Mordecai to serve as the first example of the king's purging decree?

As the gallows began to take shape, Mordecai sent word to Queen Esther informing her of the impending genocide the king had ordered due to Haman's malevolent plans. He urged her to use her influence in the king's court to inform him of the insidious plot—even if it might lead to her own death. Esther reluctantly agreed and set up a time to meet with Haman and the king.

That evening, the king had a bout of insomnia and asked that someone read to him to help him fall asleep. The chosen reading material happened to be the record books that documented all sorts of meritorious acts performed by the citizens of the kingdom. Contained within was a past incident in which Mordecai foiled an assassination attempt against the king. Xerxes asked if that deed had ever been rewarded and was told that it had not.

Perfect, he thought, I'll reward him first thing in the morning for this forgotten act of valor!

When morning came, the king summoned Haman and asked, hypothetically, how he might reward someone with whom he was well pleased. Haman, full of narcissism and vanity, assumed the king must be speaking of him. For this reason, he outlined a plan that included dressing the loyal subject in the finest royal clothes, putting him in the royal chariot, and parading him throughout the city in a massive tickertape parade.

"Great idea!" the king said. "I want you to be in charge of arranging all of that ... for Mordecai!"

There are many times in history when it would've been nice to see the look on someone's face when a script-flipping moment occurs. This would certainly be one of them.

Haman wasn't to be merely responsible for the logistics of the celebration parade, but he was required to be Mordecai's escort. To add insult to injury, he even had to shout over and over, "This is what the king does for someone he wishes to honor!" The dejection and humiliation burned at his soul. He was more determined than ever to watch his nemesis swing from the newly-constructed gallows (Side note: there is some debate about whether the instrument of torture was a gallows or an impalement pole. Most would agree that the detail is not as relevant as the fact that the condemned prisoner would face an awful and public execution).

While he was stewing in his anger and embarrassment, Haman was escorted to the palace for that dinner meeting the queen agreed to set up with the king. There, Queen Esther exposed the treacherous plot Haman had concocted and even told the king of Haman's construction of the gallows. As a result, the king ordered that the gallows' first victim would be Haman, and not Mordecai. A tragedy was averted, an injustice was made right, and a nation was saved.

When we were children we used to defiantly yell out, "Sticks and stones will break my bones but names will never hurt me."

If only that were true.

The offense of slander is denounced repeatedly throughout the Bible. Both Old and New Testaments paint a picture of a God who is intolerant of this atrocious offense. In fact, it was so revolting to God that He used His own finger to inscribe it in stone as one of the Ten Commandments: "Thou shalt not bear false witness against thy neighbor" (Exodus 20:16, KJV).

People who bear false witness against their neighbors hurt them by the lies they tell. In recent years, we've witnessed the tragic emergence of stories about teenagers who committed suicide after slanderous material was posted publicly about them on social media. Damaging activities such as this are part of the cyber-bullying dynamic that is haunting our nation's young people. No wonder the Bible correlates this activity with the wicked and even says people use slander as a weapon of destruction.

Turns out names can hurt us after all.

But slander is not relegated to our homes and neighborhoods. It has firmly taken up residency in the workplace, too. There, slander can cause all kinds of problems. As a result of its impact, people can lose jobs, credibility, promotions, the trust of peers, and sometimes worse. In my experience, slander is one of the leading causes of division among co-workers and it can lead to the premature departure of excellent employees. That's why I believe it's an important topic for this book.

No matter who you are, there may be others talking behind your back—and this can be especially true as your influence in the workplace grows, or you are successful in carrying out God's work in this world. My experience has been that the most common slanderous tool adversaries use in the workplace is lying, since it can both hurt others and promote themselves. However, there's a risk-reward relationship with slander, since lying or exaggerating to bring another down with the intent of achieving one's own rewards can backfire.

The slanderer may be a person in power who has some type of influence over us, or they have enough money and clout to slander us in order to bolster their own credibility. Other times, the slanderer might be a peer or subordinate who is seeking power. Regardless of the source, power is often a key factor in this individual's motives.

To date, I'm grateful to have had few slanderous encounters in my life and career—though I've had an unhappy employee or two. I remember one in particular who apparently succumbed to various sources of unhappiness and started an office campaign that inferred negative things about my approach to doing my job. Her messaging even included some outright lies.

Unfortunately, she was so persuasive and well-liked that some started to believe what she said and treated me accordingly. The ripple effect of these slanderous dynamics eroded relationships and trust, impacted productivity, and undermined all that I and my colleagues had worked so hard to achieve.

When I realized what was happening, I began to pray.

As my prayers continued, my eyes began to open to the spiritual attack occurring within the employee and being projected toward me. It helped me to understand that this wasn't so much a personal attack on me as it was her own internal struggle. I decided to fight on my knees and lean in on God's Word. I prayed for the .

employee, continued to show Christ's love toward her, and the situation finally resolved.

Eventually, she decided to move on to another position. Before she left, she thanked me for the years of experience and time I had sown into her. Soon after her departure, I began to receive notes of praise from her. In them, she expressed her appreciation for the training and mentoring I'd provided to her, which helped him to grow and excel in her new role. Over time, our relationship has been redefined. We're colleagues now who appreciate each other and are rooting for each other's success.

Had I taken a different approach—an adversarial or retaliatory stance—the outcome could have been much different. Instead, I chose to pray for understanding, patience, and forgiveness. I prayed for my adversary and showed her the same grace and mercy that I have received from God. Such an approach helped me to rise above the situation, and we're both better for it.

I know some readers may have had experiences much more intense and traumatic than what I've described. Those I've ministered to have included individuals who have been slandered in the worst ways—including being falsely accused of committing a crime or an act of thievery or adultery.

Regardless, slander is slander no matter what level it's on. It's painful. It hurts. And it's damaging to the person being slandered, as well as those around them.

So how do we deal with this?

First—and this may sound easier than it really is—we must know the truth internally and stand on it. Inside, you know exactly what you did or didn't do, and all truth will eventually come to light. It will always surface. Standing firm and waiting with no fear is the first, and often hardest step. It's the one that requires us to trust fully in God's justice and lean not on our own understanding. It's our opportunity to let the greatest defense Lawyer in the universe step forward to defend us and plead our case.

Next, we need to rely fully and unequivocally on God's Word to help us through the situation, remembering that this brief season will eventually pass. Whatever the source or severity of the slander, it doesn't define us, and it certainly doesn't diminish our role as God's treasured children.

We also need to resist the temptation to retaliate.

> The instinct to defend ourselves is innate, but if we lash out in the process, our behavior will be contrary to what Christ intends.

Trading insult for insult is simply not the hallmark of an ambassador for Christ. While the concept of turning the other cheek may be easier said than done, our faith can grow by leaps and bounds when we trust the Lord to fight our battles for us.

Finally, we must never underestimate the power of prayer during this season. The prayers of the righteous have moved proverbial mountains throughout history—which testifies to the fact that no request is too formidable for God. He assures us that the righteous will always be vindicated in one way or another, and our prayers in this context are a pleasing aroma to Him.

Reflection Points

Slander and blame go hand in hand, and it didn't take mankind long to discover both. They reared their ugly heads in the Bible as early as the third chapter of Genesis, when God confronted Adam after his rebellion.

When God asked Adam if he had eaten of the forbidden fruit, his first response was to blame and to slander: "The woman whom you gave to be with me ..." (Genesis 3:12, ESV).

He actually had the audacity to blame God first for his own disobedience.

Then he turned his slanderous focus on his new helpmate: "... she gave me fruit of the tree, and I ate" (Genesis 3:12, ESV).

We've been repeating this pattern and paying the price ever since.

When the heat is on, it's easy and instinctive to point a finger at someone else. To focus the attention on someone else's shortcomings rather than admit our own.

Into Action

The principle of this chapter is "Pray for Those Who Persecute You." We are all vulnerable to either real or perceived persecution in the workplace—and the manner in which we handle it is one way in which we stand out as children of God.

If you have a situation in your workplace where slander is being directed toward you, have the attitude of Christ and do not retaliate in anger. God reminds us that justice is His alone. He will take care of the situation if we thoroughly trust in Him.

The Bible provides guidance in this context in both the Old and New Testaments. For this exercise, conduct an online search for scriptural references related to the following topics, and pick at least three for each. Then pray for the Holy Spirit's insight; read through the passage; consider actually writing the passage out; and then record your thoughts and impressions. You may find more topics to research in this context as you work through Scripture, but I encourage to start with these three:

- Persecution

- God's justice

- Love

Finally, if you are the source of the slander, I am praying that something you read in this chapter will convict you to stop. Certainly, if you complete the exercise, you'll likely receive plenty of conviction about slandering someone else. It's no accident you're reading these words. The power of the Holy Spirit can help release you of this sin if you will submit to Him in humility and repentance. Will you ask for His help today?

A Prayer of Surrender

Father, I am surrounded by words of hate, and my coworker attacks me without cause. It's almost too much for me to bear. I need Your help, God, to appeal gently when evil things are said about me and not to retaliate. Just like Jesus, I will love my enemies and pray for those who persecute me, for You cause the sun to rise on the evil and the good, and You send rain on the righteous and the unrighteous.

I will not repay evil with evil; instead, I will wait for You, Lord, and You will deliver me. I will not speak evil of or quarrel with my coworker; I will be gentle and show perfect courtesy toward him/her. I won't let any unwholesome talk come out of my mouth, but only what is helpful for building others up according to their needs and for their benefit. I will be kind and compassionate to my coworker, forgiving him/her, just as in Christ, God forgave me.

Lord, You said You would bless me when people mock and persecute me, when they lie about me and say all sorts of evil things against me because I follow You, so I will rejoice! For a great reward awaits me in heaven. I will keep my conduct honorable so that when others speak against me as evildoers, they may see my good deeds and glorify God. When I am slandered, let those who revile my good behavior in Christ be put to shame, and help them surrender their lives to you.

Amen.

Scripture References

Esther 2-6

Psalm 109:3

1 Corinthians 4:13

Matthew 5:43-45

Proverbs 20:22

Titus 3:2

Ephesians 4:29

Ephesians 4:32

Matthew 5:11-12

1 Peter 2:12

1 Peter 3:16

6

WATCH THE COMPANY YOU KEEP

He that walketh with wise men shall be wise: but a companion of
fools shall be destroyed.

Proverbs 13:20 (KJV)

Elijah was the most powerful and influential prophet in the Old Testament. God routinely gave him messages to deliver to Israel's kings (Ahab, Ahaziah, and Jehoram), and usually these messages weren't pleasant. Elijah had the unenviable job of warning Israel's kings to straighten up lest they incur God's wrath. If there was ever a person who could have boldly claimed the phrase, "Hey, don't shoot me ... I'm just the messenger!" it was Elijah!

In addition to being God's trusted herald, Elijah is also known for many incredible miracles. Among the most famous were the raising of a woman's son from the dead (1 Kings 17:17-23) and calling fire down from heaven to challenge the false prophets of Baal (1 Kings 18:20-40). Elijah had such an intimate relationship with God that he actually heard God's voice on Mount Horeb

(1 Kings 19:9-14) and avoided physical death when his time on Earth ended (2 Kings 2:11).

However, being a prophet had a high risk/reward quotient. While his miracles were spectacular, there were other times when Elijah was hated and reviled. When a severe famine and drought plagued the land for over three years, people didn't think to blame it on their own disobedience and rebellion against God. It was much easier to place the blame squarely on the messenger.

Clearly, God was with Elijah, but with the many ups and downs of ministry that he encountered, he'd finally had enough. Since God was always prepared for such things, he instructed Elijah to choose Elisha as his replacement. As Elijah's close attendant, Elisha left everything to follow the prophet and learn how to pray, trust, and hear God's voice like his mentor did. Elijah trained Elisha for seven or eight years and performed many miracles in the presence of his protégé. They were together day and night and became the closest of confidants.

When both men realized that Elijah's time on Earth was coming to an end, Elisha asked Elijah for a double portion of his spirit—his anointing. Why would Elisha ask for this? Obviously, Elijah had mirrored Elisha's future to him, and Elisha wanted it. Elisha knew he could accomplish great things for God because Elijah had trained, taught, and inspired him.

After Elijah was taken up to heaven, Elisha carried on Elijah's ministry and performed twice as many miracles as his mentor had. As a prophet to Israel's kings (Jehu, Jehoahaz, and Jehoash), he's most well-known for healing poisoned water (2 Kings 2:19-22), miraculously multiplying a widow's jar of oil (2 Kings 4:1-7), making an axe head float on water (2 Kings 6:1-7), and feeding a hundred men with only twenty loaves of bread (2 Kings 4:42-44).

Another important point in this context is that Elisha was a farmer when God told Elijah to anoint him as his successor (1 Kings 19:16, 19-21). Who would have thought that a farmer would go on to perform more miracles than the man considered to be the greatest prophet in the Bible?

But when Elisha stopped hanging out at the farm and began to fellowship with a godly, anointed miracle-worker, he started to see himself and his future differently. The mentoring and on-the-job training Elisha had received from Elijah helped to ensure his success. Elijah was able to pour wisdom, strength, and understanding into Elisha because they spent so much time together. When Elisha began to mirror his mentor's life choices, this dynamic influenced his own—which set him up for a blessed and prosperous future.

Children often mirror their parents from the time they are infants until well into their teenage years. If they observe their parents treating people kindly, then it's likely they will treat others kindly. If they see their parents get angry and yell at each other, they will likely have the propensity to yell at others. If their parents are hard workers and do whatever it takes to support themselves and the household, the children will often grow up to be independent and work hard too.

In the animal kingdom, it's the same: the young mimic their parents' behavior. In both humans and animals, parents are usually role models for the children, and sometimes older siblings or grandparents serve as role models as well. Clearly, the people who surround you have a direct impact on who you become later in life.

In my own family, my parents have been my role models throughout my life. Since I come from a blended family, I was able to tap into some great attributes from all of my parents.

From my mother, I gleaned how to effectively use my talents to conceptualize a business, build it from scratch, and have the stick-to-itiveness to make it flourish. Since she was an accountant, she was strategic in all she did, and she worked hard—attributes that would define my life, too.

From my stepfather, I learned to do things in an excellent way. He was so meticulous in whatever he did—whether that was building an entire upper floor to his house, filing paperwork, or grooming our family dog.

From my biological father, I learned to appreciate the arts, value other people, love the Lord more intentionally, and enjoy the simple things in life while having fun and laughing along the way.

My grandmother was another powerful influence in my life, and she always told me, "You need to surround yourself with people who are more like you or whom you desire to be like." Then she would add, "Tell me who your friends are, and I will tell you who you are and who you'll become—so watch the company you keep."

Her words ring true to something I remember hearing along the way: that we are all composites of the five people we hang out with the most. Think of the five people you are closest to. In most cases, you will find that your salaries, your political views, your aspirations, and overall worldview are generally aligned. It's a common phenomenon that can work strongly in your favor if you choose your associations wisely—but can have a deleterious effect on your life if you don't. No wonder Proverbs 13:20 reminds us to "walk with the wise and become wise..." (NLT). In fact, the Proverbs are filled with admonitions to choose our friends wisely—and many of my favorites are listed at the end of this chapter.

I really took my grandmother's words to heart, especially in the context of those I've chosen to surround myself with professionally. In my thesis statement at NYU, I wrote about the importance of having strong mentors, especially when one is developing a career. Over the years, I've applied much of my research and writing for that project to my own life and professional career, and it has served me well.

I always knew in my heart that I was a leader because I often surrounded myself with leaders. I constantly read books and watched autobiographies about trailblazers to understand their journeys, successes, and failures. I emulated the positive things they did and tried to avoid their mistakes. I often interviewed leaders in various fields to hear their personal stories, which I found very helpful to deepen my insights. These interactions helped me build wisdom so I could avoid many of the pitfalls others my age were experiencing, especially in the workplace.

All this talk about who we hang out with reminds me of the poignant illustration of the eagle and the chickens.

There were these chickens—and strangely, one lone eagle—pecking around in a cage and doing what chickens do on a farm. One day, some eagles appeared and started flying above them. The chickens didn't think much of it, but those eagles sure got the attention of the lone eagle who was hanging out with them. He looked up at the eagles above and then down at himself and thought, "Those flying birds look more like me than these birds I'm hanging around with. Look! Their wings are not short and stubby like these birds; their wings are really long—almost seven feet—like mine."

After that day, the eagle started dreaming about being with that group of birds instead of the chickens who were content to spend their days pecking about on the farm. He dreamed of soaring through the sky and scanning the land from miles above the earth. The eagle excitedly remarked, "I want to be like them!"

So, one day he decided to just do it. He began to flap his great wings and the dust stirred into a cloud. Once he got warmed up, he flew right out of that chicken coop to join his role models so he could embrace all the benefits of being the great eagle he was born to be.

I'm sure you get the gist of that story. The eagle had been dreaming and had big aspirations. Deep down inside, he knew who he was, and he understood his potential. He knew he didn't belong in that small, confining cage, so instead of remaining comfortable where he was, he sought out birds he wanted to be like. As a result, he became successful and reached his potential.

We face a similar choice.

> We can continue to surround ourselves with
> the people who have our same problems—or
> we can choose to surround ourselves with
> those who have the solutions to our problems.

To become something greater, we need to encircle ourselves with the right people, and sometimes that can mean different people than those we are accustomed to.

By being with people we want to emulate, we will begin to understand how they think, how they feel, what they do, and why they do it. This requires intentionality, since it won't necessarily happen on its own. Often, you have to orchestrate the connection.

To that end, ever since my first real job in higher education—when I professed that I wanted to be a college president—I periodically surrounded myself with people who were in the positions that I needed to be in to reach my goals.

When I was an undergraduate student ambassador, I chose to work closely with the Vice President of Academic and Student Affairs, the Director of Student Activities, and even the president of the institution because I knew I could learn things from each of them that I couldn't learn on my own. They allowed me to shadow them and explained why they made certain business decisions and the impact those decisions would have.

While earning my doctorate at the University of Pennsylvania, I worked for the Vice President for Business Services who had a staff of more than 800 people reporting to him. He had experience that was beyond that of a typical higher education executive or administrator—he also had for-profit corporate experience.

Due to the research I was conducting there with my dissertation chair, Dr. Robert Zemsky—advisor to every sitting president since 1970—I realized that higher education was changing, and its leadership approach would have to change in order to be successful and effective. I knew it would be important to gain corporate leadership skills if I wanted to be better prepared to become a college president.

So, I learned the corporate perspective of higher education from my supervisor. He taught me how to understand profits and losses; human resources and human capital; the significance of hiring great talent; and strategic planning and outcomes measurement. It was an incredible experience.

I had a similar situation with the board chair at the college where I'm currently president. Mike Golebiowski was a successful serial entrepreneur whose primary businesses dealt with high-level technology securities in the banking system. He taught me how to truly look at a business and its management in its entirety. He showed me how to separate myself from a business in an objective way to assess it from a complete 360-degree perspective with a focus on setting goals, managing risks and outcomes, and ensuring financial viability. He often said that the numbers don't lie, and he advised me to never allow my emotions to influence important, tough decisions. He is by far one of the most forward-thinking, sincere, and benevolent CEOs (who also happens to be a devoted Christian) I've ever met. Because of his influence, I developed savvy, strategic thinking skills and became a more creative implementer.

Throughout my career, I continued connecting with positive role models, and I was able to grow by leaps and bounds because of it. I'm very thankful for the people who have allowed me to learn from them. At some time in my life, each of them mirrored the "future me" or what I wanted to become, and it has made me the person I am today.

Like Elisha, if we want to reach our potential, we must pursue relationships and positions that can provide the mentoring and training we need to prepare us for the future we desire to create. Then, we must do the same for others. We must be willing to mirror the future to someone else by choosing a protégé and paying it forward by investing in them.

Who you spend time with really does matter! In fact, it may determine the course and outcome of your life—so choose wisely. If you're a chicken, maybe it's okay to hang out with other chickens. But if you're an eagle, you were meant to fly.

Reflection Points

In Jesus' day, the highest honor a young man could have bestowed upon him was to be chosen as a disciple of a respected rabbi. In most cases, the aspiring young man would have to make the first move. He would have to formally approach the rabbi and convince him that he was a worthy candidate to be his disciple. The rabbi would then evaluate all the evidence and make the final determination of whether he wanted to take on the young candidate.

Once the agreement was made, the newly-minted disciple would immerse himself fully into the life of the rabbi. He would watch and

emulate how the rabbi did everything: how he spoke, how he react-
ed, how he read the Torah, how he cooked his meals and how he
handled his finances. It was learning through total immersion.

While traditions like those might seem a thing of the past, there's
still much we can learn from them. When we want what others have,
we must be willing to do what they have done and sacrifice what
they have sacrificed. In our microwave world, our propensity for
shortcuts has kept us from rolling up our sleeves and doing the hard
work—which is why the company we keep can be such an important
aspect of remaining focused on the plans God has for us.

Into Action

The principle of this chapter is "Watch the Company You Keep."
When we surround ourselves with the people who have the solutions to our problems or the lifestyle we aspire to, we are much more
likely to soar at their same altitude or higher. When the furtherance
of God's kingdom is a primary motivator, God can coalesce the right
people and bring them into your life at exactly the right moment. So,
make wise choices about your associations—since they could end up
defining your future.

In this context, do you know who your heroes are? Do you know
which individuals model certain behaviors you'd like to practice or
have accomplished things you aspire to?

While we may respect and admire a variety of individuals, we may
not necessarily be on the same spiritual or career path. That's why
it's important to first understand what your God-given purposes
are—so if you haven't completed the Reflections exercise in the

chapter, "Walk in Your God-Given Purpose, Not the World's" be sure to do that before proceeding with the exercise here.

If you have completed it, take your results and find individuals who you would like to emulate that seem to share similar God-given purposes. Remember, if you're seeking godly success—not worldly success—it's important to find and follow those who have done the same.

Once you have identified at least three successful individuals within this context, dig into the journey needed to achieve what they have achieved. This can help you determine next steps in your own journey to accomplish similar goals. Of course, this is a fabulous time to tap into the wisdom of a godly mentor or two who can offer valuable ongoing support to help you stay on track.

A Prayer of Connection

Father, help me to surround myself with people who are not only godly examples but also professional examples for me to align myself with. I understand that just as iron sharpens iron, one person sharpens another. I'm trusting You to bring people into my life so we can sharpen each other spiritually, professionally, and personally. As I walk with the wise, I will become wise; I will not be a companion of fools which will lead to my suffering and harm. I confess that I am blessed because I do not walk in step with the wicked or stand in the way that sinners take or sit in the company of mockers.

I will choose my companions and business associates carefully. I will not yoke myself with unbelievers, for what do righteousness and wickedness have in common? Or what fellowship can light have with darkness? I despise the assembly of evildoers and refuse to sit with the wicked. I will limit my association with people who are deceitful or hypocritical as much as it's in my power to do so.

Just as one generation shall commend your works to another, and shall declare your mighty acts, I will share my knowledge and invest in others professionally, personally, and spiritually. I will be reverent in my behavior, teach what is good, and train others how to live the good life according to Your ways, Father. I will demonstrate self-control, a good work ethic, a submissive and respectful attitude in my personal and professional life to bring honor to Your name.

Thank You, Father. Amen.

Scripture References

Proverbs 27:17

Proverbs 13:20

Proverbs 14:7

Proverbs 25:26

Proverbs 22:24-25

Psalm 1:1

2 Corinthians 6:14

Psalm 26:4-5

Psalm 145:4

Titus 2:3-5

7

WORK AND LEAD
WITH LOVE

*My companion attacks his friends; he violates his covenant. His
talk is smooth as butter, yet war is in his heart; his words are more
soothing than oil, yet they are drawn swords. Cast your cares on
the Lord and he will sustain you; he will never let the righteous be
shaken.*

Psalm 55:20-22 (NIV)

Early in my professional life, I worked for a number of major
banks. I was just emerging from graduate school during that
time and interested in absorbing every possible skill from different industries.

As you can imagine, working at a bank with all its various nu-
ances can be extremely competitive. Most of the people I worked
with were overachievers who aimed to not only reach but exceed
their goals. When the dynamics in a setting like this change—for
instance, if performance expectations are increased—the competitive environment can get even more intense.

This happened in one of the settings I worked in, and it really impacted one of the friendships I had there. As I mentioned in my earlier chapter about failure, I've never been much on making friends at work, so when I give that a shot and it doesn't work out, that's especially disappointing for me. Even so, I know God wants me to handle these situations with the kind of love He's shown me. I did so in that instance, which ended up being a really good thing, since my friend felt comfortable enough to eventually reach out and apologize for what had happened between us. If I'd acted from a position of feeling hurt, rather than a posture of love, we may not have been able to patch things up.

The lesson for me there was how important it is to show love to others we work with—including, and perhaps even more importantly—those we supervise. As I mentioned earlier, this hasn't always been easy for me, and I think I've missed a lot of past opportunities to lead with love in a way God wants me to. But these days, I'm really trying to do better.

One of my colleagues who has used this approach in leadership said she's found that when someone knows how much you care about them, everything seems to fall into place. Disciplinary issues often resolve, loyalty and the willingness to work hard typically increases, and the team as a whole works together as a much more well-oiled machine.

> When we work and lead with love, we're providing testimony to God's love for each of us, and sharing it in a practical way.

However, it's not always easy to work or lead with love especially as we're trying to maintain professional boundaries and performance expectations. In that context, working from a posture of love doesn't mean being a pushover who won't hold others accountable. Instead, it means loving them enough *to* hold them accountable to be the best they can be and providing the guidance and support necessary to help them do that.

Honestly, my experience with my former coworker wasn't just disappointing—it really hurt at the time, because I thought we were close. Through experiences like that, I've gained a deeper appreciation for what it must have been like for David in his relationship with King Saul. As I mentioned in an earlier chapter, things often got dicey between the two of them—since King Saul's insecurity and self-interests made him quite a fickle king for someone who achieved success as easily as David did.

David went to extraordinary lengths to serve King Saul well. When he was a mere shepherd boy, Saul heard about the beautiful music David played and summoned him to the palace to soothe Saul's tormented soul. Undoubtedly, David must have felt it was a huge honor for the King to request that he play his harp. Because of the relief Saul felt when David played, the king was very pleased and asked him to stay and serve in his court. Saul loved the precocious young man very much and even promoted him to the prestigious position of armor bearer.

Unfortunately, David had no idea that Saul wasn't the sugar he appeared to be—instead, he was salt.

As soon as David tasted success by killing Israel's fiercest opponent, the giant Goliath, everything between David and Saul changed. No one else in all of Israel had the guts to face Goliath much less defeat him until David (who was just a teenager at the time) came forward and bravely announced he would fight the giant. David certainly distinguished himself from the rest of the frightened army—and he was just getting started!

Saul began to hate David for the success he enjoyed and the public praise he received. But David was clueless about the king's festering ill will, since he assumed Saul would be ecstatic about his defeating Goliath and slaying the rest of the Philistine army. Instead, the insecure Saul felt jealous and threatened, and became particularly enraged when the women from the towns sang, "Saul has slain his thousands, and David his tens of thousands" (1 Samuel 18:7). As a result, Saul began to obsess over the idea that David would soon take his throne.

And why wouldn't he?

One might agree that David had it going on! He was good-looking, talented, brave, successful, and admired by the entire nation. David's success was obvious, and the reason behind it even more so: God was with David. Even Saul recognized that the young man's success was because of God's hand upon his life, but instead of being happy for David, he was envious.

Maybe that was because he knew the same wasn't true for him. Even though God had chosen Saul to be the first king of Israel, he'd made some very bad decisions that resulted in God withdrawing His approval and His hand of blessing. God was no longer with Saul, and his soul was tormented because of it. So when he recognized that God was with David, Saul became afraid of him.

As a result, Saul's mind went to some very dark places. He actually wanted to kill David and tried to do just that on several occasions. Though David must have been perplexed as to why all this was happening, he eventually realized that his life was in danger and fled to the mountains to hide. David mourned his broken friendship with Saul and wondered why his king would treat him so cruelly. He cried out to God and leaned on Him for protection, never forgetting God's promise to make him king someday.

For many years, David hid from Saul, waiting for God to fulfill His promise. During that time, God was actively working in David's heart. He developed a strong, intimate relationship with God while he was running for his life, and God taught him many important lessons in the wilderness that would help him be a better king than his predecessor.

Despite being unjustifiably slotted for the king's hit list, David wasn't full of hatred and anger toward Saul. If anything, David felt sorry for the king and empathized with how tormented and unhappy he was. David's heart wasn't full of bitterness and resentment toward his enemy because he had God's perspective—and His heart. That's why he was able to forgive his persecutor and move forward with grace. This set David up to become a great leader who was known for being a man after God's own heart. Because David refused to seek revenge, wallow in bitterness, or harbor resentment, God honored him with so much success that even enemy nations developed a healthy respect for him.

The truth is, when we walk with God and enjoy success like David, sometimes people will resent us and friends will abandon us. Those who do apparently don't understand that, because God is with us, we walk in His favor and blessings. Sadly, instead of rejoicing with us, they may feel jealous or even threatened by our success.

Like David, when we experience betrayal or abandonment by a friend because of our achievements, we have a choice. We can feel hurt and withdraw while indulging in resentment, or we can allow God to work within us as we seek His perspective about the situation. Either way, God will honor us when we choose to forgive, refuse to let bitterness set in, continue to love our enemies, and show them grace.

Reflection Points

"If you love only those who love you, why should you get credit for that? Even sinners love those who love them!" (Luke 6:32, NLT). Jesus' words must have been stinging as he challenged the crowd with this irrational concept: Love people, even when they don't love you.

These words remain antithetical today when our tendency is to cozy up to those who are sympathetic to us and eschew contact with those who might disagree or have a different philosophy from our own.

Other people can be the source of great pleasure—and great pain. Relationships will fail us repeatedly in the course of our lifetimes. Friends may turn to foes, and sympathizers may turn to adversaries.

However, in the midst of such unpredictable dynamics lies a solid, immutable truth: God is the same yesterday, today, and forever. And

He is calling us to a life of peaceful existence with others (Romans 12:18).

~~~~~~

Into Action

The principle of this chapter is "Work and Lead with Love." In this context, it's important to take responsibility for our relationships to ensure we're operating from the foundation of love to which God calls us. This can be especially challenging when we don't feel loving toward someone else for one reason or another. However, being able to love others as Jesus has loved us is essential if we are to be witnesses for Him in the workplace.

For this exercise, consider taking responsibility for your part of a difficult relationship. Although you may also have them in your personal life, here, I'm talking about those which are related to work. However, since problems in our personal relationships can trickle into work and vice versa, you may end up deciding to attend to those, too.

Start by identifying work relationships that need this kind of attention by asking yourself the following questions:

- Is there someone for whom you harbor resentment for one reason or another?

- Have you done something within this relationship for which you owe an apology?

- Are you willing to show love for this person, even if you don't get any back?

Next, pray over your responses and ask God for His help in treating this person the way you would like to be treated if you were on their end of the stick. Once you receive God's guidance about what next steps are needed, ask for His help and timing in resolving your part in things.

This healing process is applicable whether the individual is a peer or someone you supervise in some way. When the latter is the case, you can learn to lead with love while maintaining professional boundaries and performance expectations as you do. Since supervisors possess the ability to influence things positively or negatively for those they supervise, it is important to lead with love as a testimony of your faith in the workplace.

A Prayer of Protection

Father, I'm hurting because I've been deceived, and I feel betrayed. Please give me wisdom about how to handle this situation with my friend/coworker and to honor You at the same time. Save me, Lord, from lying lips and deceitful tongues. You promised that a false witness would not go unpunished, and whoever pours out lies would perish. So, I will trust You, God, to expose the lies, vindicate me, and plead my cause. I know You will rescue me from those who are deceitful and wicked.

I will remember that everyone who wants to live a godly life in Christ Jesus will be persecuted, and that evildoers and impostors will go from bad to worse, deceiving and being deceived. Yet I will watch out for and avoid those who cause divisions and mislead me. God, You will help me to discern those who lie and speak with flattering lips from a deceitful heart.

As far as it depends on me, I will live peaceably with everyone. I will be kind to those who betray me, just like You were, Jesus. I won't be overcome by evil; I will overcome evil with good.

I am determined to love my enemies and do good to those who hate me. With Your grace, I will bless those who curse me and pray for those who hurt me. I will be still in Your presence, Lord, and wait patiently for You to act. I will not worry about evil people who prosper, nor will I fret about their wicked schemes; I will rest in God's peaceful presence.

In the name of Jesus. Amen.

Scripture References

Psalm 120:2

Proverbs 19:9

Psalm 43:1

2 Timothy 3:12-13

Romans 16:17

Psalm 12:2

Romans 12:17-21

Luke 6:27-28

Psalm 37:7-9

8

HONOR WHAT OTHERS INVEST IN YOU

But he that received seed into the good ground is he that heareth the word, and understandeth it; which also beareth fruit, and bringeth forth, some an hundredfold, some sixty, some thirty.

Matthew 13:23 (KJV)

The Sea of Galilee can be quite the enigma. When the lake is calm, it's one of the most serene places on Earth. But because of the way it's geographically situated, almost completely surrounded by mountains, shifting wind patterns can change the tranquil body of water into the most horrifying nightmare without much notice.

It's the lowest freshwater lake on the planet, and while it has supported a significant commercial fishery for more than two millennia, on some days it yields its bounty extravagantly, and on other days it stubbornly refuses to share with the most persistent fisherman.

It might be poignant, then, that Jesus chose this as the backdrop for one of his most enduring parables. With the mountainside acting as a natural auditorium of sorts, Jesus told the story of a farmer who scattered seed into his land. Some of the seed fell on highly fertile soil, some of it fell on less-fertile soil, and some of it fell by the wayside. When the seed that had taken root began to germinate, some did so at an average rate, and some got choked out by weeds and thorns. But the seed that fell on the highly fertile soil experienced a hundred-fold explosion of growth!

Later, when Jesus was pressed to explain the meaning of the parable, He told His disciples that the seed represented God's Word, which would be deposited into people's hearts in a variety of ways. Some of it would find a fertile host, and some would be rejected entirely. Jesus was teaching His disciples a valuable lesson regarding the way heavenly deposits can yield much fruit—or may be entirely discarded, depending upon the receptacle.

In a previous chapter we talked about how mentors are critically important in our lives and how they play a critical role in helping to shape who we become. In this chapter I want to expound on that, because while it is good to have a mentor, it is equally important to know how to optimally interact with this individual and balance his/her expectations with your own.

Good mentors do one of two things for you: They either deposit a seed into you, or they water a seed that has already been deposited by the Lord or someone else in your life. The role of a mentor is very specific and unique to each person. The goal of this relationship is to help you find and remain on the path God has for you as a means of achieving your purpose here on Earth. Many people obtain the services of a mentor, but they may not truly understand how to make the most of the relationship.

As we delve deeper into these ideas, I have a key question for you: When dealing with your mentor, are you an oven or a garbage can?

I know that might sound a bit bizarre and perhaps a little frivolous. To help you understand what I'm referring to, let's look at the structure and dynamics of these two objects.

Typically, food that is placed in the oven is some version of uncooked and will be baked, broiled, or warmed. However, it eventually transforms into a prepared dish that provides nourishment and promotes life.

For example, as a child, I loved to eat lasagna, so it was one of the first dishes I learned to make when I left home. However, before making it, you must buy the right ingredients—including beef or turkey, cheese, sauce, and spices. And lasagna just wouldn't be lasagna without its foundation—those big flat noodles with curls on the sides.

Then, each item has to be positioned and layered just so if one expects it to bake and transform into that mouth-watering dish of pasta, sauce, and melted cheese I grew up with. If any of the ingredients are missing or the creative techniques lacking, the lasagna will likely fall apart, be inedible, or not provide the intended nutrition.

Now let's examine the use of a garbage can.

Like the oven, the garbage can is also a receptacle. We throw away waste, discard things we don't need, or get rid of items that no longer serve a purpose. In the kitchen, after we throw out food that spoils quickly, it begins to rot and creates an awful stench that permeates the environment around it. Before long, we have to collect the bag, tie it up, and toss it into a larger garbage can outside so it can be taken away.

Now, let's compare the two examples.

When food is placed into an oven, this receptacle transforms it into a tasty, nourishing meal. In fact, the aroma of the dish can provide pleasure for an entire neighborhood while the food itself provides sustenance to everyone sitting at the dinner table. When things are placed in an oven, there's a spirit of expectation that something great will result after a determined period of time.

On the other hand, when you deposit something into a garbage can, you do so because you have no expectations for its further use or purpose. Things in a garbage can have been deemed unneeded. You would never put something valuable or useful there with plans to retrieve it later.

Consider how your parents, co-workers, and ministry leaders have made positive deposits into your life. What have you done with them? Have you nurtured and used them to produce something significant? Do they create a pleasing aroma and nourish all those around you? Or have you allowed them to sit inside you and rot, relegating them to a future of uselessness and disposal?

In this context, are you an oven or a garbage can?

I cherish those people who have deposited valuable things into my life that built me up spiritually and encouraged me in my walk with Christ, as well as in my ministry. From the time I was a little girl in Catholic school, I was being built up spiritually without even realizing it. In reality, I spent a lot of spare time at church.

At a young age, I volunteered at St. Clare School in New York, which was part of my church. There were altar boys at the church, but not many altar girls. I was proud to have been chosen to be an altar girl, and the priests and nuns were excited to have young students to work alongside them and to mentor. During those times, we were taught that we were God's children and that we were special. We were told how to behave in a Christ-like manner, to love God and our parents, to be kind to others, and to excel in school. Little seeds were planted in me then, adding to those my praying grandmother and grandfather had originally planted in me.

After I graduated, my mom enrolled me in a Catholic, all-girl, no-nonsense high school that was run by nuns. My physics teacher had multiple degrees; she was strict and incredibly intelligent. Her teaching, mannerisms, and behavior were always impressive and professional. I asked her many questions about physics and about life and she was always gracious about taking the time to answer. By doing so, she awakened my ability to think critically about both natural things (like physics) and the supernatural things of God.

Over the years, other pastors, ministry leaders, and sisters in Christ deposited treasures into me. I can't name them all, but I thank them wholeheartedly. There is, however, one person I need to mention who has spent an inordinate amount of time mentoring me and helping me become the bold, Christian professional that I am today. That's my spiritual father, Dr. Bill Winston, pastor of Living Word Christian Center near Chicago, Illinois.

Dr. Winston is a highly decorated veteran, pilot, former IBM executive, author, and serial-entrepreneur whom God called to preach the gospel throughout the world and to minister to the poor and sick. He cares deeply about educating the next generation and has a heart for serving God's children. Having created successful businesses, schools, innovation centers, and church plants from the ground up, he is a visionary in every sense of the word.

What I admire most about Dr. Winston is that he boldly professes what he believes to others all around the world: that Jesus Christ is Lord and that putting faith to work is paramount. He is a mouthpiece for Jesus Christ and a valiant soldier in God's army. Many of Pastor Winston's attributes are noteworthy and worth modeling.

Due to the valuable time he has invested depositing his knowledge and passion into me, I have become stronger and more confident in expressing my own God-given abilities. He has helped me to dream bigger, and I cannot thank him enough for the treasures he has deposited into my life. However, while communicating my admiration is important, my gratitude can best be expressed by nurturing and multiplying those deposits to produce something valuable from them.

One of the most critical things I've learned from being both protégée and mentor is that we must not take for granted what our mentors sow into us. We don't want to waste their time or our own.

> When others invest in us, we have an obligation to take what they've given us, develop it, and allow it to grow into something useful and fruitful that nourishes everyone around us.

I've been blessed to have other soldiers and ministry leaders—like Dr. Marilyn Hickey—pour into my life, as well. She opened up her home to me and spent hours sharing about her successes and failures in ministry, her relationship with the Lord, her love for people of all races and creeds, and how to be the best Christian I can be. As a result, I grew exponentially in my spiritual life and in my ministry. I will never forget her generosity, love, openness, and sincerity.

Anne Graham Lotz, the daughter of Dr. Billy Graham, is another mentor. I invited Anne to be the keynote speaker at our annual GCPWA conference. The attendees of that event are still dissecting and talking about her presentation and how it broke strongholds, brought people to Christ, and changed lives. During our time together she encouraged me, prayed over me, invited me to stay in touch with her, and sent me a beautifully uplifting letter of acknowledgment for the work I do with GCPWA. She thanked me for allowing her to be a part of our conference, and I was truly touched by her kindness.

Over the years, I've realized the need to be an oven rather than a garbage can. Of course, discernment is essential—since ungodly or negative deposits should be tossed in the trash. But when those deposits are a good thing, we should operate like an oven by developing the positive, godly seeds that are placed within us.

When people spend their precious time investing in us, they desire (and deserve) to see the fruits of their labor. What a delight for a mentor to witness their nurturing efforts resulting in something magnificent that advances God's Kingdom. This has been true in my life, and it's certainly true regarding you and your mentors, too.

The Apostle Peter is a great example of being both an oven and a garbage can—since he routinely alternated between the two. Peter started out as one of Jesus' three closest confidants among the 12 disciples. He always seemed to be right in the middle of the action because he didn't want to miss a thing. Convinced that Jesus was the long-awaited Messiah, Peter gave up everything to follow Him.

Over the course of three years, Jesus mentored and trained Peter and the other disciples about God's kingdom, His love, and His plan. Though Peter and the other disciples often missed the deeper truths Jesus was trying to instill in them, Peter scored high points for at least trying to be an oven. While Jesus often taught in parables and said things that sometimes didn't make sense, Peter tried valiantly to grasp the more profound meanings of his mentor's teachings.

But Peter is also well-known for being the disciple who repeatedly put his foot in his mouth—like the time Jesus shared that He would be killed in Jerusalem. What was Peter's response? He took Jesus aside and rebuked Him. Did you catch that? Peter rebuked Jesus! Say what you want about this fisherman's lack of knowledge, but he certainly made up for it with his arrogance! However, the Master wasn't impressed.

Jesus turned and said to Peter, 'Get behind me, Satan! You are a stumbling block to me; you do not have in mind the concerns of God, but merely human concerns.' (Matthew 16:23, NIV)

How would you like the Son of God to call you "Satan"? Yikes.

Later, Peter promised to follow Jesus to the death, but ended up denying Him three times instead. Apparently, this wasn't the most promising internship.

On the other hand, Peter's confidence and temerity resulted in his being the only human being who would ever know the thrill of walking on water with Jesus. Clearly, Peter did his best to learn from Jesus and develop the treasures He was depositing into him.

But that all changed when Jesus was crucified.

After Jesus died, Peter's dreams of change and emancipation for the Jewish people died, too. He'd thought things would turn out in a predefined way, and he was shocked when they didn't. Along with so many others, Peter believed Jesus would conquer the Roman oppressors and that Israel would enter into its golden post-Messianic age. Although God had bigger plans— salvation and victory for the entire world—Peter didn't know that at the time.

Surprisingly, even though Jesus appeared several times to the disciples after His death, things just weren't the same. With nothing panning out as he had hoped, Peter probably felt like a failure for denying Jesus. By his estimation, Peter had let his master down and likely viewed himself as a worthless disciple. And there's only one thing to do with something when it's worthless: you throw it into the garbage can. So, instead of embracing everything Jesus had taught him, a discouraged, garbage-can-minded Peter returned to his previous employment: fishing.

But Jesus remembered all He had deposited into Peter. That's why every parable, every miracle, and every promise over the past three years was about to culminate into yet another lesson for Peter: Jesus wasn't finished with him yet.

In John 21, Jesus reminds Peter that he was in fact called to be an oven. Yes, Peter had made mistakes, but Jesus had deposited much truth and wisdom into him, and Jesus knew Peter would play a herculean role in the development and growth of the soon-to-be-born Church.

After this time with Jesus, the first few chapters in Acts provide the account of a renewed, oven-minded Peter who steps up fearlessly to take on a definitive leadership role. Later, when the Holy Spirit descended on him and the other believers in the Upper Room, Peter was so filled with God's power that he preached an inspiring, Earth-rattling sermon that resulted in 3,000 new believers in one day! (Acts 2:14-41)

Peter had finally stepped into his true purpose and was operating as an oven, not a garbage can. All the teachings and truths Jesus deposited into Peter started turning into a great harvest that powerfully and fearlessly advanced God's kingdom. Peter bounced back from his shortcomings as a disciple and parlayed them into one of the most profound turnabouts in history. From fisherman to preacher. From failure to leader. From coward to miracle-worker. From hopeless to hope-dispensing. From the garbage can to the oven.

Since Peter was so instrumental in the growth and success of the Church, what would've happened to the Body of Christ if Peter had failed to step up and be the leader God called him to be? What if he missed his rendezvous with destiny and allowed the cold and empty reality of the garbage can to overtake the fragrant and transformative reality of the oven? God's plan for His church would certainly have unfolded either way, but Peter would have missed out on the adventure of a lifetime—and of an eternity.

Now it's your turn. Your choice. Will you choose to develop the seeds that have been planted in you by your mentors so that you can make a positive impact in this world? Or will you throw them away? Your mentors are cheering you on. A desperate world is waiting. And God is watching with hopeful anticipation.

Reflection Points

God has sown seeds of greatness in you. That's not even debatable. It's simply fact. Throughout your life, He has continued to make certain deposits in you. Perhaps it was through a divine meeting He set up for you. Maybe it was through a specifically-targeted message that was for your ears only. Or possibly it was through a position of influence He afforded you. These seeds, strategically deposited, could be ignored, marginalized, trampled upon—or carefully watered. The choice is yours.

But the results are yours as well. If you choose to ignore gifts and talents God has given you, you'll likely end up living in mediocrity. But if you choose to water the seeds and commit to finishing what God has started, He can change the world through your influence.

~~~~~~

Into Action

The principle of this chapter is "Honor What Others Invest in You." In that context, pay attention to the mentors God has placed in your life. In all likelihood, they have been strategically placed there to move you toward your destiny. For this exercise, please take a few moments to:

- List the mentors you believe God has placed in your life.

- Describe the specific deposits they have made into you.

- Describe how you have been honoring these investments by nurturing them and helping them grow.

- Take time this week to send a note of thanks to each of these mentors and let them know how their investments are bearing fruit.

Remember, your mentors want to reap a harvest as well. They want to see the seeds they have placed in you grow a hundredfold. They have a vested interest in your success. Don't ever take for granted these treasures God has placed in your life. They have been specifically chosen to help guide you along the path He has set before you. Thank Him today for His careful provision for your life and your destiny.

Prayer of Proclamation

I confess that I am a trustworthy steward. Since I am faithful and wise, the Lord can trust me to be a leader in His Kingdom, and people can trust me to lead faithfully at home and in my job. As I am faithful in small and large assignments, God and other people will trust me with greater responsibilities. And as I am trustworthy with worldly wealth, God will trust me with the true riches of heaven.

Whatever I do, I will work heartily, as for the Lord and not for people. I will embrace the gifts God has placed inside me, serving others with the strength He provides, so that in all things God may be praised through Jesus Christ.

I will not think of myself more highly than I ought, but rather I will think of myself with sober judgment, in accordance with the faith God has distributed to me. In His grace, God has given me gifts for doing certain things well, so I will use these gifts for His glory, whether it be prophesying, serving, teaching, encouraging, giving, leading, or showing mercy.

Father, you have given me specific spiritual gifts by Your Spirit, and I will apply these gifts to benefit others. I won't squander the gifts You've place in me, rather, I will step fully into them so I can benefit my family, my church, and my workplace. I trust that You will give me faith, wisdom, and knowledge as I walk in the gifts You've instilled in me.

In the name of Jesus, amen.

Scripture References

1 Corinthians 4:2

Luke 12:42

Luke 16:10-11

Colossians 3:23

1 Peter 4:11

Romans 12:3-8

1 Corinthians 12:7

9

USE YOUR CREATIVITY TO SOLVE PROBLEMS

In the beginning God created the heaven and the earth. And the earth was without form, and void; and darkness was upon the face of the deep. And the Spirit of God moved upon the face of the waters. And God said, Let there be light: and there was light.

Genesis 1:1-3 (KJV)

For as long as I can remember, I've been creative. I was an incredibly curious child and wanted to know how things worked—which meant my mind often wandered while I tried to figure things out. Although my second grade teacher thought I was daydreaming in class and told my parents as much, that was never the case. Instead, I was quite present while she was teaching, but also thinking about many other things.

For example, if the teacher was talking about the significance of the invention of the airplane, I was simultaneously wondering about the technology needed to construct it and which birds the inventors studied to design it. But to my teacher, I was doing nothing more than daydreaming.

So, I'm a dreamer. Guilty as charged—and proud of it, too. In fact, I would dare say that those who dream are often those who achieve great things because they can see beyond the norm.

It's a fond habit of mine, this dreaming that I do. I find myself frequently pondering how something can be done differently to improve a situation—like that time I was eight years old and too tired to get out of bed to turn off the light. Wouldn't it be amazing if I could just clap my hands and turn it off? I thought to myself.

Well, apparently someone else thought the idea was amazing, too—and applied their creativity to create a mechanism that did exactly what I envisioned. By doing so, they made life better for a whole host of individuals who needed that kind of convenience and likely became quite wealthy in the process. Perhaps the Lord provided the inspiration behind the idea, and perhaps not. Either way, imagination and creativity were applied to solve a problem that needed to be addressed.

Throughout my life, others have counted on me to be a problem solver—whether that was in my community; at school, church, or work; or with my family and friends. I loved to figure out ways to work more efficiently and effectively—like the tools I developed for memorization and the techniques I used to get my homework done with more speed and accuracy.

When I served in student government at my undergraduate college, I created clubs that helped to solve problems students faced and bridged gaps with the administration. These clubs supported students in building leadership skills, provided valuable volunteer experience, and taught them how to have clean fun on campus. When my efforts caught the attention of the president of the college, I was promoted to student ambassador. In this role, other capable students and I were the eyes and ears for the administration, sharing ideas that could help improve things at the college. My creative streak continued through the remainder of my undergraduate years and during grad school.

As I transitioned into my professional life, I took that mentality with me and utilized as much creativity as possible in my job. There, I was able to identify problems quickly and offer unique solutions to resolve them. In my early work years, I was blessed to have supervisors who appreciated me and gave me the freedom to make such recommendations—which were often implemented. Their support made me feel valuable and contributed to my confidence and sense of self-worth.

It was incredibly rewarding to witness how my input positively impacted the organizations I cared about. This dynamic has helped to inform my approach to leadership, since subsequent promotions resulted in more responsibility and opportunities to have an even greater impact on the divisions I was directly overseeing—and even the company as a whole.

As a result, others started to view me as both a problem solver and a major contributor to help organizations enhance and achieve positive outcomes. At the broader organizational level, I developed new business processes and homegrown technology that improved methods for presenting critical data so key stakeholders could understand it more easily. This helped to optimize data-informed decision making that supported risk mitigation and organizational success.

At the employee level, I found ways to consolidate jobs, and—rather than firing those who were struggling—I often created alternate solutions that helped them apply their specific abilities more effectively. This approach created a win-win for the employee and the organization, since by doing so we were able to maximize an individual's potential while concurrently cutting costs.

Early in my career, I was faced with a major challenge that introduced me to the world of being a turnaround manager. One of our country's most prestigious universities was experiencing a precipitous decline in enrollment within a specific program and I was hired to determine why that was and what could be done about it. Since this particular program enjoyed a stellar reputation, the change was baffling.

Was there a waning interest in the field? Were peer institutions gaining more market share? Was it something internal—like a lack of quality customer service from the enrollment team or processes that were outdated or nonexistent? Was the decline somehow related to the school's reputation?

Since the situation was a bit dire, I was limited to a few short months to assess what factors—both internally and externally—might be working against the school. It didn't take long to identify two major culprits: ineffective marketing to prospects and inefficient processes within the school.

However, since the school already had a trailblazer-reputation, a unique and creative approach to addressing these problems would be needed, instead of settling for the status quo. We didn't want to be like other schools. We wanted to embrace creativity and innovation to improve marketing and the handling of internal affairs.

So, I conducted some research, formulated my ideas, and presented them to members of the decision-making team—who wholeheartedly supported them. Once these solutions were implemented, interest in the school quickly gained ground. The phones started to ring, applications from qualified students picked up, and we ended up both meeting and exceeding our goals.

As I completed this assignment, I began to understand the power of using creativity in the workplace for the first time in my career—and was rewarded with a promotion and a sizable increase in pay.

While all of that was a great early start, I've found much more success and satisfaction within the context of innovative thinking as I've increasingly incorporated the Lord and His principles into everything I do. In this context, I've been inspired by God's early leaders, like the prophet Daniel.

Daniel knew all about the power of using his God-given creativity to solve problems and secure his future. An exile taken from his homeland, Daniel was chosen from among the brightest young people in the land to take part in three years of rigorous training so he could work in the king's service. Although living in a foreign land involved learning about the laws and customs there, Daniel refused to forsake his own godly beliefs and convictions in the process.

For starters, Daniel refused to eat the regular food offered to all the chosen young men because it had probably been offered to idols and this directly contradicted his faith. When he asked that he be given only vegetables and water instead, his request was denied because the king's official didn't want to get in trouble. He was certain Daniel and his Hebrew friends would look sick and malnourished if they didn't eat the royal food.

But this didn't stop Daniel.

> Nothing could stop Daniel, instead of giving up, he offered a creative solution to his persecutor.

"Please test your servants for ten days: Give us nothing but vegetables to eat and water to drink. Then compare our appearance with that of the young men who eat the royal food, and treat your servants in accordance with what you see" (Daniel 1:12-13, NIV).

Since Daniel honored God by putting his faith first, God caused the king's official to favor Daniel and his friends. He accepted Daniel's creative offer, and after ten days, Daniel and his friends looked healthier and stronger than all the other young men.

As a result of his faithful stance, God blessed Daniel and his friends and they enjoyed the respect of the king, since "In every matter of wisdom and understanding about which the king questioned them, he found them ten times better than all the magicians and enchanters in his whole kingdom" (Daniel 1:20, NIV). Their spiritual anointing led to the promotion of Daniel and his friends into the king's service because they were viewed as assets who could benefit the kingdom with their wisdom, understanding, and creativity. Daniel's story is the perfect example of the fact that promotion is often the result of creative problem solving.

During King Nebuchadnezzar's reign, Daniel showed himself to be an incredibly creative problem solver—and no problem seemed bigger at the time than the king's recurring nightmares. Many sleepless nights had caused the king much anguish. His dreams were filled with symbolism he couldn't decipher and he was desperate for answers. In his despair, the king called all the magicians, enchanters, sorcerers, and astrologers hoping that one of them could solve this problem for him—but all to no avail. In his great frustration, the king decided to kill all the "wise men" of the country because apparently they weren't very wise at all—and this included Daniel and his friends.

Again, Daniel refused to go down without a fight. When the commander of the army came to kill Daniel and his friends, Daniel sweet-talked him: "When Arioch, the commander of the king's guard, had gone out to put to death the wise men of Babylon, Daniel spoke to him with wisdom and tact" (Daniel 2:14, NIV).

Daniel convinced Arioch to allow him to approach the king and try to solve the problem. But first, Daniel and his friends sought God's face and asked for mercy and wisdom to understand what the king's dreams meant. And God didn't disappoint. That very evening, God revealed the mystery of the dream to Daniel through a dream of his own.

The next morning, Daniel confidently approached Arioch and—before delving into any explanations—he interceded on behalf of the unsuccessful wise men who were condemned to death. He asked for a stay of execution since he was about to give the king the information he so desperately sought.

When brought before Nebuchadnezzar, Daniel proceeded to tell him in graphic detail exactly what he saw in his dream and offered him an equally detailed explanation of what the dream meant. Of course, he gave God all the credit for his unique insights.

King Nebuchadnezzar was dazzled and fell prostrate on his face before Daniel, acknowledging that Daniel's God was surely "the God of gods and the Lord of kings and a revealer of mysteries…" (Daniel 2:47, NIV).

In this amazing moment, God received the glory because Daniel relied on Him to solve this problem. The eventual result of this? Daniel was promoted…again! The king "made him ruler over the entire province of Babylon and placed him in charge of all its wise men," (Daniel 2:48, NIV) and the king gave him many gifts for a job well done. Even more, since Daniel had earned significant influence with the king, he confidently requested that his friends be given positions as administrators, and the king quickly obliged.

Daniel's story and my own experiences are prime examples of the fact that when you solve problems with God's help, you'll likely find that people favor you, trust you, and promote you. Remember, when you put your faith first and seek God for His wisdom, He'll empower you to be a creative problem solver, too.

Reflection Points

You may not always feel like the most creative person on the planet. I get it. But remember that you were created in the image of the Almighty God, and He is the most creative Problem Solver of all time. As God's image-bearer, it's your birthright—your heritage—to embrace creative problem solving wherever you are and in whatever you're doing.

~~~~~~

Into Action

The principle of this chapter is "Use Your Creativity to Solve Problems." If you invite God to become involved in this process and expect that He will give you the creative solutions you need as you reflect His image to those around you, you'll be astounded about how He can use you. In that context, take a few minutes to:

- Describe a difficult problem in the workplace that has you stumped.

- Go back and read the story of Daniel in this chapter, and consider his example of involving God in this process.

- Like Daniel, ask God for His wisdom regarding the situation.

- Brainstorm and describe the creative solutions that come to you as a result of seeking God's help.

- Then write out the next steps needed to embrace the creative solution He shows you.

- Repeat this process and apply it to problem-solving situations as needed.

If God did it for Daniel, He can do it for you. God is looking for those who will take the time to seek Him and will give Him the glory as the greatest Problem Solver of all.

A Prayer of Creativity

God, in the beginning, You created the heavens and the earth. How manifold are Your works! In wisdom have You made them all; the earth is full of Your creatures. And because You created me in Your own image, I am full of creativity and able to solve every problem that comes my way. As I seek You to find innovative solutions to problems, I will incorporate Your principles into everything I do.

I am God's workmanship, created in Christ Jesus for good works, which God prepared beforehand, that I should walk in them. It is my destiny to be a creative problem solver so God receives the glory. I am filled with the Spirit of God, with skills, with intelligence, with knowledge, and with every creative ability to solve the problems I face in both my personal and professional lives.

God's Word prepares and equips me to do every good work. In any matter requiring wisdom and balanced judgment, I am fully capable to offer prudent counsel. Like Daniel, I am filled with the Holy Spirit and with His insight, understanding, and wisdom; I am filled with supernatural knowledge and understanding and can solve difficult problems. As I solve problems with God's help, people not only give glory and praise to Him but they also favor me, trust me, and promote me. As I put my faith first and seek God for His wisdom, He will empower me to be a creative problem solver.

In the mighty name of Jesus. Amen.

Scripture References

Genesis 1:1

Psalm 104:24

Genesis 1:27

Ephesians 2:10

Exodus 35:31

1 Kings 3:12

2 Timothy 3:17

Daniel 1:20

Daniel 5:11-12

10

BE PREPARED FOR THE OPPORTUNITIES AHEAD

Watch therefore, for you do not know what hour your Lord is coming. But know this, that if the master of the house had known what hour the thief would come, he would have watched and not allowed his house to be broken into. Therefore you also be ready, for the Son of Man is coming at an hour you do not expect.

Matthew 24:42-44 (NKJV)

There probably isn't a greater illustration of preparedness in the Bible than John the Baptist. Every aspect of his life was about being prepared. In fact, some seven centuries before he was even conceived, the prophet Isaiah foretold of John's birth and essentially predestined him to a life of preparedness by heralding him as the forerunner to the coming Messiah (Isaiah 40:3).

This shadow of preparedness started with John's father, Zechariah. When the angel of the Lord appeared to him (Luke 1:5-23), Zechariah was told to prepare for fatherhood. At his age, this pronouncement appeared to be a ridiculous assertion, and his fleeting doubt earned him a nine-month bout with laryngitis.

Nevertheless, the angel's declaration was resolute: Prepare to have a son. Prepare to keep him abstinent from alcohol. Prepare for his influence to have far-reaching effects throughout eternity. And most importantly, sit back and watch as your son prepares the way for the Redeemer of the world.

John seemed to take his impending mission so seriously that even in utero, he couldn't help but remind those around him that he was going to kick and scream every time he had the opportunity to be in the presence of his Lord (Luke 1:41-42).

As John grew, it's likely his parents shared what the angel foretold and urged him to get ready for the purpose God had planned for his life. As parents often do, they probably admonished him regularly to be diligent and focused in preparing for the mission ahead. However, it was up to John to prepare himself accordingly so he would be ready when the opportunity appeared.

To do so, John jumped in with both feet. In early adulthood, he removed himself from the distractions of everyday city life and relocated to the only place he could have true solitude: the wilderness. It was there that the majority of his preparation occurred as he grew in knowledge of the Scriptures and learned to commune more deeply with God.

In fact, John's desire to prepare the way of the Lord was so complete that he gave up the conveniences of regular life—including typical food and typical clothes. He ate insects and wore animal skins instead of wasting time on frivolous distractions. He knew that being prepared required extreme discipline, so he was willing to go far beyond what most were willing to do. Even today, this type of mindset is what separates the unprepared from the prepared; the unsuccessful from the successful; the good from the great.

Perhaps John also used his time in the wilderness to sharpen his teaching skills. If so, the fact that his audience was limited to rocks and cacti likely didn't matter, since the practice helped him be ready to stand before others and deliver those fiery sermons he was known for about the need for repentance and salvation. John's ministry was effective because he was filled with the power of God, and he did what was needed to be prepared to fulfill his mission.

While being prepared can ready us for what's expected, it can also help us to pivot more easily when the unexpected occurs. While John was baptizing the multitudes at the river, he looked up and scanned the crowd—which was probably a habit of his. In one unexpected moment, his gaze fell upon a solitary figure who was standing at the back of the line.

Aside from the meeting between John's mother Elizabeth and Jesus' mother Mary when they were both pregnant with their sons, we are not told of any other interactions between Jesus and John. In fact, John 1:31 seems to indicate they'd never met in person before Jesus stepped into that line. But John had probably envisioned it all the days of his life—fantasizing about what it would be like the day he'd come face-to-face with the Savior of the world.

Though the moment had finally arrived, it wasn't at all what he'd imagined.

When Jesus stepped forward and assumed the position of one preparing to be baptized, it threw John for a loop. This was not at all what he'd expected. What was he to make of this? The Creator of the universe—the One who'd spoken everything into existence—was requesting baptism from one of His creations? Preposterous!

Though John was initially taken aback, his preparedness and keen understanding of the Scriptures meant he was able to pivot and embrace this very unexpected turn of events as he submitted joyfully to Jesus' request.

John's example of preparedness is one we can all follow. An old saying provides a key equation in this context: Preparation + Opportunity = Success. Too many are unsuccessful in their endeavors because they lack preparation or they miss an opportunity—and these two issues can play a big role in keeping individuals from advancing in their careers.

In my own life, I've developed the habit of thinking ahead to prepare for the future by setting goals and developing a plan for achieving them. For instance, from the time I was young, I knew I wanted to be in the field of education and planned to be a teacher. But my time working for the school superintendent while I was in high school honed that focus a bit and I decided to become an administrator, instead.

During my college years, I developed a fascination with and passion for all things relating to colleges and universities. Since I was a student ambassador, I was able to shadow the president of my college. By doing so, I learned a great deal about higher education from both the student and administrative perspective and decided to follow that path.

I was so impressed with the president of my college. She was the first female to hold the presidency post in the history of the State University of New York. Like her, I wanted to be in charge and have a positive impact on both the students and the field of higher education as a whole. As a result, I decided to work toward becoming a college president and started to develop my plan for doing so.

My plan included a determination to be as prepared as possible so I would be ready when my opportunity arrived. I read leadership books and self-help books; took classes to help me understand how to read and interpret financial data, budgets, and profit and loss statements; and I participated in internships. I challenged myself to hone the skills I already possessed and build those I lacked.

In one of my roles, I realized that to truly be competitive in my presidential quest, I would need to have experience in academic affairs—so I secured a position to help me gain it. I connected with those could help me to obtain the practical experience I needed while also preparing myself educationally for my future role. I also began to dress and act in a way that aligned with both the leadership mentality and leadership roles I wanted to embrace. And I did the leg work—reading books, case studies, interviews, and reports regarding issues related to college presidency. Ultimately, it all paid off and I eventually became a college president.

How did I attain my goal? It started with discovering God's purpose for my life and then changing my mindset so I could embrace it. I asked Him for His direction, began to think on purpose about my future, and refused to let life just happen to me.

If you want to achieve your goals and dreams, I'd encourage you to do likewise. First, discover God's purpose for your life, and then ask for His help in working toward achieving that which aligns with it.

In one of my positions, I had an administrative assistant who did exactly that. She had been there for many years, and was highly competent in every aspect of her role. She was well respected and everyone enjoyed working with her—including me. Since I'm committed to helping those I work with achieve their goals, I regularly ask those I supervise about their goals and how I can help them get there. When I asked my administrative assistant this question one day, she expressed an interest in an advanced role for which she would have been a great fit. Not long after, this exact type of position opened within our department, and I encouraged her to apply and then put in a good word for her with the hiring manager.

Several weeks later, when we learned that she didn't get the job, we were both baffled and disappointed. However, the deciding factor ended up being her lack of a college degree—which was specifically required for this role.

However, instead of languishing in her disappointment and giving up, this determined woman went back to school and finished her degree. It took three years to do it, but when the same position was posted at a later point in time, she was grateful to have done the hard work of preparation to secure it the second time around. Her preparation met opportunity, and she enjoyed the successful outcome of getting to step into her dream job at last.

That's what preparation does. It readies us for both the expected and the unexpected.

It also gets us through seasons of push-back and limited support. In the case of John the Baptist, some balked at his fiery message and deemed him a radical kook, while others responded with enthusiasm by repenting and getting baptized. Regardless of the response, John was determined to continue preparing the way for the coming Messiah, even though he wasn't sure exactly when the Messiah would come. Such a commitment to preparedness allowed John to pivot quickly and obediently when the time was right.

The same thing can happen to each of us. When an opportunity appears in a way or at a time that isn't what we envisioned, we must be ready to act, which is especially true today. We are living in a time of great opportunity in which your spiritual and professional goals can flourish—if you will take the time needed to ask God for His direction and then prepare yourself accordingly.

Reflection Points

If you were to ask 100 people who they thought the greatest person was to ever walk the face of the earth (excluding Jesus Christ), you'd likely get a varied list of names spanning the generations like Moses, King David, Joseph, The Virgin Mary, Mohammed, Albert Einstein, Buddha, Mother Teresa, and a host of others.

However, nestled away in Matthew 11:11 is a stunning, often over-looked verse in which Jesus proclaims the winner of this honorary title: none other than John the Baptist. This astounding declaration should encourage each of us to aspire to such greatness by emulating those who came before. John's greatest attributes were his faith, his obedience, and his preparedness.

Into Action

The principle of this chapter is "Be Prepared for the Opportunities Ahead."

You may have read my words in the preceding paragraph and thought to yourself, "I'm no John the Baptist." But when John came face-to-face with Jesus, he essentially said "I'm no Messiah-baptizer." Yet all the days of his life John had been preparing to be exactly that—he just didn't know this specific detail of God's plan. Fortunately, when all of his relentless preparation culminated in a critical moment of opportunity, John was ready for it.

How about you? When your critical moment of opportunity arrives, will you be able to say the same? For this exercise:

- Take time in prayer and study of the Word to seek God's guidance about the type of preparation you should be focusing on within this season of your life.

- Write down your perceptions about the guidance you receive.

- Assess your current efforts to determine whether they align with this guidance.

- Discuss your results with a godly mentor or trusted advisor.

- If adjustments are needed in your focus, ask God to help you decide what those are and how to proceed.

- Watch with anticipation for the opportunity God will provide—and step into it with joy, knowing it's what He's been preparing you for all along.

- And don't forget to share your story with others who need encouragement along similar lines!

A Prayer of Preparation

Lord, I won't just hope for the right opportunities to come my way; instead, just as the horse is prepared for the day of battle, I will diligently prepare myself to be ready for whatever You bring my way. I will be a faithful steward of Your grace by using the gifts You have created in me to serve others and advance Your Kingdom. I am determined not to become weary in doing good, for at the proper time I will reap a harvest if I do not give up.

I will prepare my mind for action and exercise self-control, fixing my hope completely on Jesus and His purpose for my life. I confess that I am His workmanship, created in Christ Jesus for good works, which God prepared beforehand so I would walk in them. I thank You in advance for the opportunities and open doors to witness to others and expand Your Kingdom in both my professional life and my personal life.

I will patiently wait for Your timing, God, being ready at any opportunity to complete the assignment You give me. Thank You for giving me the opportunity to know the secrets of the kingdom of God; help me to clearly see, hear, and understand how to prepare myself for the future opportunities You already have planned for me. I won't be afraid to step through the doors You open for me because I proceed with Your wisdom and expect that with You by my side, I will enjoy great success.

In the mighty name of Jesus, we pray. Amen.

Scripture References

Proverbs 21:31

1 Peter 4:10

Galatians 6:9

1 Peter 1:13

Ephesians 2:10

Luke 21:13

John 7:6

Luke 8:10

11

ACHIEVE MEGA INFLUENCE BY SHARING A MEGA VISION

And the Lord answered me, and said, Write the vision, and make it plain upon tables, that he may run that readeth it.

Habakkuk 2:2 (KJV)

God was the first mega visionary. First, He envisioned creation, then in Genesis 1, He created the heavens and the earth according to what He envisioned. Then He created man to oversee and manage His creation. Since we were created in God's image, and we have God's DNA, it's our destiny to be creative visionaries, too.

So what exactly is a visionary?

> A visionary is a person who thinks about or plans for the future with imagination or wisdom. But more importantly, a good visionary paints a picture of the future so effectively that others will become passionate about it, too.

Let's unpack that for a moment.

Naturally, most of us think about the future—how we would like to live, where we would like to work, what type of car we would like to drive. But how many actually plan for the future with imagination and wisdom? Too many live day-by-day with no real plans for their lives or their futures. In fact, it's not uncommon for someone to spend more time planning a summer vacation than they do laying out a plan for their lives!

Alternatively, there are others whose plans help to change people's lives, develop industry, and impact the world. I call such individuals mega visionaries. Like Albert Einstein, Queen Esther, and Martin Luther King. These kinds of visionaries had dreams and visions for change that may have been inspired by God or perhaps just a sense of discontentment with the status quo.

Visionaries are driven by the need to solve problems and some of the most impactful visions and subsequent changes start with a place of need. In this context, when a problem rears its head, the visionary is able to step up and offer ideas that can make things better.

Visionaries are leaders in every way. They travel unknown territory to either create something new or improve upon that which is already in play. A visionary has the faith and ability to make the invisible become visible and to envision things that don't yet exist as if they already do.

As I've shared with you in this book, I started vividly daydreaming when I was in grade school, and I continued daydreaming throughout most of my life. But once my eyes were opened to God's Word, and I began to meditate on it, I understood that I wasn't daydreaming at all; I was having visions. I've been able to see myself in certain professional positions well before I reached them.

However, visionaries need another key component to be successful: the other people God places in their lives. Leaders and visionaries cannot accomplish what they envision without help. Visionaries must have others' financial support, labor, enthusiasm, and passion. They need the help of those around them to back the vision and bring it to life.

Additionally, visionaries must be able to convey a vision that others sometimes can't see themselves. I cannot begin to imagine what it was like for the Wright Brothers to conceptualize such an undertaking as designing and developing an airplane from scratch. To execute their vision, they first had to convince someone to finance the idea, and then they had to persuade the world to buy into it. Today, the implementation of their vision means we have faster ways to transport people from one place to another—and can even spread the Gospel more easily throughout the world.

If you are leading a group of people, you must cast a clear vision regarding your future plans for that group. Paint a picture of the future that creates such passion in them that they will hardly be able to contain themselves. Lead the charge. Help them "see" what can happen as the result of fulfilling this vision. They need to know you have a clear picture of what the future may hold and a plan for helping them achieve it.

Obviously, a leader without a vision and supporting plan can't be very effective. Can you imagine getting on a boat and discovering that the captain of the ship doesn't know where he's going? Or how he's going to get there? Or if he doesn't know how many crew will be needed or what type of equipment will be required? What would happen to this boat? It would never reach its destination. It would drift aimlessly with no clear purpose, and everyone on the boat would be lost. No wonder Proverbs 29:18 tell us that without a vision the people perish.

Leaders often have a blueprint for their vision. They write down the vision in the form of a concept paper or strategic plan that outlines the mission and defines the goals, strategies, and outcomes along with how to measure successful implementation.

Likewise, when you have a mega vision, it's important to clearly communicate it so people can understand it and rally around it. As a visionary, your job isn't simply to see what is possible; you also must be an influencer to help others see what is possible. A mega influencer. You must be able to persuade others to do what is needed in order to carry out a vision they may not be able to see themselves. In fact, don't be surprised if others think you're crazy and that your vision makes no sense. Remember, while you can see it as though it were real, they may not be there just yet.

Jesus was the greatest visionary who ever lived. He came into this world with a purpose that was laid out by his Father in heaven. And while He knew what He had to do, His path was not always clear regarding how He was going to do it.

Yes, that's right: like us, Jesus was a student, too. Hebrews 5:8 tells us that Jesus even learned obedience through His sufferings. Through it all, Father God was the influencer in Jesus' life, and Jesus' job was to influence the multitudes to help them enter into a relationship with His Father—which was a radical concept at the time.

In my many leadership roles over the years, I've been blessed to get to lead more than 1,000 employees. I've led them through great times of growth, innovation, and excitement—but I've also led them through challenging and uncertain times: job retrenchment, revenue shortfalls, massive restructuring, uncertainty regarding the future of the organization, September 11 attacks, the COVID-19 pandemic, and everything in between. I've been a consultant for many leaders whose organizations needed assistance with vision-casting and sometimes with executing that vision.

In having had the privilege of doing all of that, I've found that the most important aspect of being a visionary is the ability to get others to buy into what you're asking them to do. Otherwise, the vision will never be fulfilled. I've also found that people buy into visions that are clear, have an impact, and allow them to contribute in a valuable way.

A great leader must also be passionate about the vision and confident that there will be positive outcomes. People want to believe that a leader can take them to the "promised land," and they rally around servant leaders who have great integrity and character. A servant leader is someone who is willing to be in the trenches with the people they're leading. They serve them in any way that's needed to help clarify the vision, maintain work-life balance to accomplish the vision, and provide the training needed to carry it out.

In one of my positions, I inherited a very large office with windows on a main city street. When I realized I didn't need so much space, I decided to turn it into a center for learning and excellence. The center was designed from the need to accelerate learning and to build a holistic environment for students. Today, it is the only concept of its kind at a college in the Midwest.

Within that project, I didn't just direct activities; I helped staff move furniture, clean up the space, and complete other odd tasks. I performed those activities along with my team; I never asked the team to do something I wasn't willing to do myself. In short, I did my best to lead by example. People are willing to follow a visionary who not only expresses a clear vision but who also exhibits the traits of a leader who will able to get them from point A to point B successfully.

Finally, it is important for a visionary to develop a track record of success. The more a leader's visions are accomplished, the easier it will be to get buy-in from others. Fact, everyone who follows a visionary must be able to trust that the final outcome will be one of success.

Being a visionary can be a very lonely existence, but God can mightily use those who stay the course—like Joseph.

Joseph's story begins when God gives him a vision of his future, and he dreams that his father and brothers will bow down to him one day. As you can imagine, when Joseph shares this grand vision his family, they aren't the least bit impressed. In fact, they're angry and assume Joseph thinks he's better than any of them. Now obviously, Joseph could've shown more discretion here, but he was just a teenager when God gave him these visions. In his exuberance and youthful passion, he simply blurted what God had shown him without contemplating the potential consequences or how that would make his family feel.

As the story continues, Joseph's brothers decide to rid themselves of their little visionary sibling. Genesis 37:19-20 reads, "'Here comes that dreamer!' [the brothers] said to each other. 'Come now, let's kill him and throw him into one of these cisterns and say that a ferocious animal devoured him. Then we'll see what comes of his dreams'" (NIV).

Joseph's brothers faked his death and sold him to some slave traders who took him to Egypt. But God was with Joseph and caused Potiphar, one of the most influential men in Egypt, to buy him. Even in his Egyptian master's house, Joseph proved himself to be a visionary. Joseph found favor in Potiphar's eyes because God gave him success in everything he did. Genesis 39:4-6 says, "Potiphar put [Joseph] in charge of his household, and he entrusted to his care everything he owned. From the time he put him in charge of his household and of all that he owned, the Lord blessed the household of the Egyptian because of Joseph. The blessing of the Lord was on everything Potiphar had, both in the house and in the field. So he left in Joseph's care everything he had; with Joseph in charge, he did not concern himself with anything except the food he ate" (NIV).

Joseph was able to get Potiphar, the captain of the Egyptian guard, to buy into his vision, and Joseph was wildly successful. Unfortunately, Joseph was falsely accused of betraying Potiphar and was thrown into prison. But once a visionary, always a visionary. Joseph didn't allow his less-than-ideal situation to kill his vision.

"While Joseph was there in the prison, the Lord was with him; he showed him kindness and granted him favor in the eyes of the prison warden. So the warden put Joseph in charge of all those held in the prison, and he was made responsible for all that was done there. The warden paid no attention to anything under Joseph's care, because the Lord was with Joseph and gave him success in whatever he did" (Genesis 39:20b-23, NIV).

Again, Joseph was able to influence others because of his ability to see what others could not, and they bought into it. As a result, everything at the prison ran smoothly thanks to Joseph. Thankfully, Joseph didn't remain in the prison forever. After God gave him the ability to interpret the dream of Pharaoh's cupbearer, Joseph was eventually called to the palace to interpret Pharaoh's dream. God gave Joseph the interpretation of Pharaoh's dream which prophetically told what the future held for Egypt and the surrounding area.

Joseph explained that Pharaoh's dream foretold a coming famine that would last for seven years. Because Pharaoh was amazed at Joseph's interpretation and wisdom, he asked Joseph what should be done to preserve their nation. Joseph laid out an extensive plan to save and store food over the next several years.

Genesis 41:37-40 reads, "The plan seemed good to Pharaoh and to all his officials. So Pharaoh asked them, 'Can we find anyone like this man, one in whom is the spirit of God?' Then Pharaoh said to Joseph, 'Since God has made all this known to you, there is no one so discerning and wise as you. You shall be in charge of my palace, and all my people are to submit to your orders. Only with respect to the throne will I be greater than you'" (NIV).

Joseph cast vision in Potiphar's house, then in the prison, and finally in Pharaoh's palace. Later, Joseph's brothers (the ones who sold him into slavery) came to Egypt to buy food because they and their families were suffering from the famine—which is when his dreams of his brothers bowing down to him came true. Ultimately, Joseph's vision influenced Egypt's leaders to follow his plans and directives. And as a result, his visions and the courage to follow them save him, his family, and an entire nation.

What if Joseph had given up when he was in the prison? What if he had ignored the visions God gave him for the future? Many lives would have been lost, including his own family's. In the same way, we cannot ignore the dreams and visions of the future God plants in us—because he wants to use us to make a difference in this world.

Like Joseph, will you clearly cast your vision and then influence others to help you accomplish it? If so, you'll be able to improve and bless many lives and bring glory to God at the same time.

Reflection Points

Imagine if Martin Luther King had kept his vision of a desegregated and racially unified nation to himself. Imagine if the clear picture he had of black and white kids playing together, of Jews and Gentiles communing together, and of the descendants of slaves and former slave owners sitting together at the table of brotherhood had simply remained in the recesses of his overly-active imagination. The march on the National Mall would have never happened. A movement would have been stopped dead in its tracks. Millions of marginalized people would have looked into a bleak future without a glimpse of hope.

But visionaries, by their very nature, can't do that. They can't hold it in. Even Jeremiah, the "weeping prophet," said that if he tried to contain the vision God placed in his heart, it would be like fire in his bones. "I am worn out trying to hold it in! I can't do it!" (Jeremiah 20:9, NLT).

Into Action

The principle of this chapter is "Achieve Mega Influence by Sharing a Mega Vision." When God places a vision in your heart, it's your duty to make that vision known and to spearhead the effort to execute it. Although God could have chosen anyone to do that, He specifically chose you. For this exercise, consider the four points I discussed in this chapter. As reminder, they can be summarized as follows:

- The most important aspect of being a visionary is the ability to get others to buy into what you're asking them to do.

- A great leader must also be passionate about the vision and confident that there will be positive outcomes.

- People rally around servant leaders who have great integrity and character.

- It is important for a visionary to develop a track record of success.

In this context, consider your own leadership practices and how they align with what I've described. For this exercise, instead of sitting down and writing things out on your own, ask a trusted colleague or two who works with you—both peers and those you supervise would be great choices—to rate your efforts within each of these four points. An important aspect of the selection process is to pick those who are thoroughly familiar with your visionary habits and will be honest with you about how they are perceived. Completing this exercise can help you determine if you're ready to be the mega influencer and mega visionary God called you to be.

A Prayer of Vision

Father, as a leader and an influencer of people, give me an understanding heart so I can lead them well, and help me to know the difference between right and wrong. I desperately need Your wisdom to cast the vision You've given me for this organization. As I seek You, give me Your vision for the people and organization I lead; help me to write it, to present it, and to make it plain to everyone on my team. I will not be afraid to speak and I will not be silent about the vision You have given me for this organization.

As I lead, I will speak the Word of God and the vision of God to those over whom I have authority. I will conduct myself in such a way that others can imitate my faith, ethics, and integrity. I will be above reproach, faithful, temperate, self-controlled, respectable, hospitable, teachable, and able to instruct. I will do nothing out of selfish ambition or vain conceit; rather, in humility, I will value others above myself and consistently empower and lift them up to fulfill their purpose.

I will be approachable and caring in the way I relate with my coworkers. Like a good shepherd, I will pay attention to their condition and will be sensitive to their needs and preferences. Like my Creator, I will creatively and carefully lead the people He's entrusted to me in the way we should go so we can all be successful together.

Praise the Lord! Amen.

Scripture References

1 Kings 3:9

Proverbs 29:18

Habakkuk 2:2

Acts 18:9

Hebrews 13:7

1 Timothy 3:2

Philippians 2:3

Proverbs 27:23

12

BE A CHAMPION FOR CHRIST IN THE WORKPLACE

For I am not ashamed of the gospel of Christ, for it is the power of
God to salvation for everyone who believes....

Romans 1:16a (NKJV)

It can be common for professionals and entrepreneurs who embark upon a journey of personal development to experience spiritual awakening in the process. That may occur as the result of a chance meeting, a personal crisis, or an intrinsic desire to find greater meaning or purpose in life. As their faith develops, these professionals often yearn to cultivate their spirituality in ways that enhance both their personal and work lives. Additionally, they may desire to impact the communities in which they serve with their faith.

However, despite the universal positives of a vibrant, selfless faith, the incorporation of spiritual beliefs and practices is still largely unaccepted, particularly in workplace settings. Often, Christians are not encouraged or empowered to practice their faith in the workplace or at their place of business, so they may not feel comfortable doing so. Such discomfort may be related to fears about losing their jobs or facing victimization at work. Entrepreneurs may be afraid they will lose employees, potential partnerships, patrons, and even revenue if they choose to express their faith and Christian values.

For these reasons, many believers tend to leave their faith at the front door of the work setting. By doing so, these "closet Christians" fail to advance God's Kingdom for fear of persecution or ostracism.

Does any of this sound familiar? If you're not sure whether you fall into the closet Christian category, consider the following questions:

When asked to share about yourself at a meeting, at a networking event, during an interview, or in friendly conversation, do you mention that you're a Christian?

In your cubicle or office, is the Bible displayed among the books, magazines, journals, and newspapers you have in open view on your desk or bookshelves?

When difficult conversations arise around religious topics, values, or ethics in which your views would be the minority perspective, do you profess your faith and stand for what you believe and value in Christ?

If you answered "no" to at least one of these questions, then you may, indeed, be a closet Christian.

I was once one, too. However, when I became aware that I was hiding my faith at work, I felt obligated to make a change. As Christians, we are called to operate from a place of love and a sound mind, not of fear. The Lord has equipped and empowered us to take dominion over all the things of the earth—including our workplaces—to be champions for Him. That's why it's time for us to quit leaving Jesus at the office door only to reconnect with Him on our way out. In my life, when I started bringing Jesus into my workplace, amazing things began to happen.

Over the years, I made it a habit to pray, study God's Word, spend time in fellowship with the Lord, and talk about God during off-hours. Occasionally, I began to carry out those practices at work when I started feeling more comfortable with who I was in the workplace and particularly when I understood my identity in Christ. However, I became most comfortable openly exhibiting my love for Christ, my faith, and my relationship with the Father when I began working as the chief executive officer of my college. I felt responsible for shaping the organization's mission and culture and for ensuring that it had a strong foundation that would allow all stakeholders to grow and benefit.

As the president of an institution of higher learning, I've naturally felt responsible to support those who have a desire to realize their educational dreams. However, I wanted to take that a step further by helping to ensure that our stakeholders—including students, faculty, and staff—were groomed and trained in a holistic manner.

At the college, we facilitated various types of seminars and workshops designed to build our students, faculty, and staff from a professional or academic standpoint; however, we did not focus on building them up spiritually (which is understandable given that we are not a Christian institution). In spite of this, I felt it was important to help people grow spiritually, since I believe that for a person to be whole, every facet of their being should receive the needed attention—especially the spiritual component.

Although I had a desire to bring my Christian faith and values into the workplace, I wasn't sure how I would accomplish it. With the various laws related to the separation of church and state, I knew it would be a challenge. Now don't get me wrong, I had been personally practicing my faith in various ways at work for some time, but it wasn't something I wore like a badge of honor on my chest. If someone asked me about my faith, I would gladly and enthusiastically share, but it wasn't information I volunteered on a regular basis.

One way I had practiced my faith through the years was to pray with others when needed. Over time, I started noticing that people were showing up at my office for prayer on a more regular basis. As a result, I grew more comfortable with who I was as a Christian. When I finally decided to be more public about my faith, I did so boldly and without fear. I knew I had been placed in a position of great influence, and I wanted to carry out my duties with God as my guide so I could be a light for Him to all those around me.

During one of our board meetings, I asked the trustees if it would be permissible for me to host on-campus Bible studies for anyone who was interested. I assured them the meetings would not be held during class time and wouldn't interfere with normal campus activities. To my great joy, they approved the request, and I started holding a weekly time of prayer and Bible study at 7 a.m. on Wednesday mornings—which we fondly referred to as the Hour of Power. Sometimes, we met in the evenings or on weekends, instead. The meetings evolved from being gatherings attended only by students and grew to include faculty and staff, too. Over time, our Hour of Power flourished as God blessed our efforts to encourage one another in the faith.

Another way I've practice my faith has been to spend time prior to the start of each semester and during exam weeks walking the campus and praying over the classrooms, hallways, and offices. One day, one of my staff members saw me doing this and smiled. Soon after, she came in very early one morning with her holy water (she was Catholic) and began to anoint and openly pray. Our actions started spreading like wildfire and people who were not Christian began to come to know Christ.

Lots of other amazing things started happening once I decided to incorporate Christ into my workplace. For starters, my days were more peaceful and extremely productive. I had a sense of clarity and felt confident in my decision-making. The heavy workload and responsibility of my position felt lighter because I was making godly decisions and setting policy that reflected my core beliefs and values. I was able to impact and change lives for the better, and in turn, those individuals were better equipped to have a positive influence on their families and communities.

At the same time, our enrollment numbers began to grow exponentially—by as much as 20 percent year-over-year. This fact in itself was impressive enough, but it occurred during a period in which the country was emerging from a recession and other institutions of higher education were experiencing major declines in enrollment. Additionally, our balance sheets started tipping in the right direction—from a deficit in revenue to a tremendous surplus at the end of the fiscal year. It was unimaginable…and supernatural!

As a result of all of these dynamics, the entire culture of the institution changed. Our outcomes drastically improved; our people seemed happier and more productive; and even our meetings were more pleasant as a result of bringing Christ into the workplace. Everything was better!

Even more, I was better. I felt more at peace with the Lord, knowing that I was being faithful to Him in every area of my life. This also translated to the members of our board, who were impressed by the positive outcomes we had achieved. They gained confidence in my leadership abilities and rewarded me accordingly.

As Christians we are called to share the good news about Jesus Christ, but many of us struggle to do so. Why is this? Why is it so easy to share good news about a restaurant we enjoyed, a great movie we watched, or an exciting sale at a department store—but not the good news of our Lord? As I mentioned earlier, some level of fear is often the culprit.

However, once we do step out and start sharing, we often learn how contagious enthusiasm can be. I was so excited about what was going on in my life and in my workplace; about how my entire environment was changing; and about how God was working in people's lives that I was compelled to share it with everyone I knew—especially my fellow professionals. These professionals (who also happened to be my friends) wanted to know how all that could be. How could I practice my faith at work? A common response to my sharing went something like this, "You mean to tell me that your boss allowed you to talk about God on the job? I'm so afraid that I might lose my job if I did that."

The truth is, anyone can do what I did. Anyone can be a champion for Jesus by being bold enough to live their faith in all areas of their lives—including work. Of course, Christian champions in the workplace must adhere to labor laws and honor certain stipulations to remain in compliance. But even in this context, I found that when I started sharing my experiences and practices with others, they, too, began to do great things through Christ in their work settings.

A prime example of this is my younger sister—who also embraced the idea of bringing faith to work. I regularly shared everything I was doing at the college and in other areas of my life, and she literally ran with it. She had just completed ministry school (which is certainly not a prerequisite for bringing faith into your work environment) and was working at an elite gym at the time.

In her role there as a personal trainer and experienced nutritionist, my sister often met with clients who were looking for positive change in their lives—including their physical health and appearance. As she developed a physical workout and eating plan for them, she talked about her love for the Lord and how she maintains her strong and fit body because it's the Lord's temple and she treasures it. As a result, she was sometimes asked to share more about her faith and about the Lord, so my sister did exactly that—and even led some to Christ. It's no surprise she exceeded her membership goals! I'll never forget the day she told me that with the permission of her supervisor, she did her first baptism in the pool at the gym. Now, that's a champion!

Of course, I'm not saying we all should perform baptisms in our workplaces, but wherever we are in our jobs, our communities, and our businesses, we're in a position of influence. Even more, God has specifically placed us there to be influential for Him. We need to understand that as business owners and professionals, we are called to effect change through Christ because we are on assignment for God. As Christ followers, our purpose should be to use our God-given talents to create positive change in our environment, advance God's kingdom, and share the love, hope, and good news of salvation through Jesus Christ.

I hope you can sense the passion I have for this topic. Writing this chapter is exciting for me because the very essence of what I stand for involves this point: as professionals, we have a responsibility to bring Christ into our workplace, to help others grow closer to the Lord, to make godly decisions, and to apply ourselves with excellence through Him.

When I received this revelation from the Lord—that He is raising up a group of soldiers for Christ who are professionals, and many of them are women—I was compelled to launch the Global Christian Professional Women's Association (GCPWA), which now connects over 30,000 women in more than 55 countries worldwide.

GCPWA has given me the opportunity to travel nationally and internationally and to preach, teach, consult, and train others about bringing Christ into the workplace. It's clear to me that this is what the Lord has called me to do and that I am walking in my purpose—and you can do the same.

> Whatever you're doing, you can do it even
> better by incorporating Christ *completely* into
> your life.

Stop being a closet Christian and watch the blessings shower upon your life and the lives of those around you.

In an earlier chapter, I discussed the biblical account of Esther, primarily through the lens of Mordecai. But this short book also provides a fantastic example of a woman who found herself in a place of influence in a foreign land. And at the right time, she revealed her faith in God and helped save many people from annihilation.

In Esther 1, we read that King Xerxes ruled over 127 provinces from the Middle East to India. After a falling out with his queen, he decided to choose a new queen. He brought hundreds of beautiful virgins to his palace, gave them beauty treatments for a year, and then summoned them one by one into his personal chambers. Whichever young woman enchanted him the most would become his new queen.

Esther was a young, Jewish orphan being raised by her uncle, Mordecai. She was one of the women selected to compete in this ancient "beauty pageant." Before she left home, Mordecai gave her strict orders not to share her family history or heritage with anyone since Jews were often looked down upon. Almost immediately, Esther set herself apart from all the other women. Esther 2:8b-9 reads:

«Esther also was taken to the king's palace and entrusted to Hegai, who had charge of the harem. The girl pleased him and won his favor. Immediately he provided her with her beauty treatments and special food. He assigned to her seven maids selected from the king's palace and moved her and her maids into the best place in the harem" (NIV).

God's favor was clearly on Esther's life because she honored Him. Hegai not only gave Esther the best treatment but likely gave her inside information about how to win the king's heart and how to stand out from the crowd. Esther understood that if she wanted to be chosen as queen, she needed wisdom and advice from those who knew the king. Esther 2:15 says:

"When the turn came for Esther ... to go to the king, she asked for nothing other than what Hegai ... suggested. And Esther won the favor of everyone who saw her" (NIV).

Clearly, as Esther was being groomed to potentially be the next queen, she worked in an excellent manner and conducted herself in a way that caused others to honor and favor her. It paid off because King Xerxes chose Esther to be his queen. And even though she didn't broadcast to everyone that she was a Jew and a follower of Jehovah God, the way she lived her life displayed her faith every day.

After a time, an honored royal official in the king's palace named Haman plotted to kill all Jews in the land because of his deep hatred for them. He told the king that the Jews disobeyed the laws of the land and persuaded the king to draw up an edict calling for their annihilation. King Xerxes assumed Haman's request was for the good of the nation and agreed with Haman's plan.

When Mordecai found out about the edict, he informed Esther and begged her to speak to the king about it. Esther wanted to help, but she was afraid to approach the king uninvited and possibly be sentenced to death for doing so. Mordecai replied, "Do not think that because you are in the king's house you alone of all the Jews will escape. For if you remain silent at this time, relief and deliverance for the Jews will arise from another place, but you and your father's family will perish. And who knows but that you have come to your royal position for such a time as this?" (Esther 4:13-14, NIV)

Mordecai was challenging Esther to step into her calling and take a stand for her faith and her people. Esther asked Mordecai and all the Jews to fast with her for three days. Then she said, "When this is done, I will go to the king, even though it is against the law. And if I perish, I perish" (Esther 4:16, NIV). After fasting and praying, Esther approached the king and eventually exposed Haman's evil plan. She told the king that she herself was Jewish and begged him to spare her people.

In the end, Esther's actions led to the salvation and rescue of the Jewish nation. She put her own safety aside because her people were counting on her to save them. She used her position to influence the king to make decisions that favored the Jews, and the king complied.

As you can see, Esther was a fearless woman who lived for God and boldly made decisions that glorified Him. She used her God-given talents to navigate through difficult moments, keeping God first in all her ways. In the end, she was greatly rewarded for her actions both in the natural and the spiritual, and multitudes of people around her—even those whom she did not know—benefited from the fact that she walked in faith in her place of influence.

But what if Esther had been a closet believer? What if she had remained silent when she could have spoken up? Many lives would have been lost, and Esther wouldn't have fulfilled her purpose for being in that royal position.

We, too, must remember that when God puts us in a place of influence, it's not for us—it's for Him and others. It's to advance His purposes and kingdom and to save people from spiritual destruction. We can't afford to be closet Christians. There's too much at stake. Like Esther, we cannot shrink back in fear or intimidation. Instead, we must resolve to invite Christ into our positions of influence so we can better reach those who so desperately need Him.

Reflection Points

This little light of mine, I'm gonna let it shine.

Remember that little jingle that many of us first learned in Sunday school? It's catchy and cute, to be sure, but it's loaded with spiritual dynamite. The concept is simple but the spirit behind it is profound.

In Matthew 5:15, Jesus ponders the absurdity of having a light and then placing it under a bushel. Lights, by their very nature, are meant to be seen in the fullness of their expression—and our lives are no different. Our identity in Christ is meant to be worn like a badge pinned to our chests, not like a membership card nestled in our wallets.

Although the workplace dynamic can be tricky, too many Christians tend to pre-judge or to assume what others might say or how a supervisor might react if they openly professed their faith. As such, they often hide that light under a bushel and never allow the fullness of Christ's light to glow.

～～～～～～～～～～～～～～～～～～～～～～～

Into Action

The principle of this chapter is "Be a Champion for Christ in the Workplace." This week, I encourage you to take a risk. Let your light shine at your workplace through your words and through your actions. You don't have to be obnoxious about it, but let people know where you stand when an opportunity arises. In all likelihood, it will not be as negative as you might anticipate. In fact, you may end up planting seeds that will grow a hundredfold and gaining a level of respect you didn't know was possible.

But most importantly, you will have fulfilled your calling and responsibility as a champion for Christ in the workplace.

A Prayer of Commitment

Thank You, Father, for Your gift of salvation, which is by no means a reward for the good things I've done. Rather, I know You did not save me by Your grace just so I could go to heaven; I am Your masterpiece, and You have created me anew in Christ Jesus, so I can do the good things You planned long ago for me to do. I will be Your messenger, Lord; I will go for You—send me!

You have put me in this position for such a time as this, and with Your help, I will rebuild, repair, and revive the people and the organization in which You have given me influence. You have chosen and appointed me to bear fruit in this organization for Your Kingdom, so let my fruit remain; thank You that whatever I ask the Father in Jesus's name, He will give me.

I vow that whatever I do in my workplace, whether in word or deed, I will do it all in the name of the Lord Jesus, giving thanks to God the Father. With Your grace, I will be the salt in my workplace that stirs up a thirst for the things of God; I will be the light that cannot be hidden, shining the love of God to everyone I come in contact with. I will not be afraid to share my faith; I will always be prepared to give a gentle, respectful answer to everyone who asks me why I have such hope, joy, and peace.

Amen.

Scripture References

Ephesians 2:8-10

Isaiah 6:8

Esther 4:14

Isaiah 61:4

John 15:16

Colossians 3:17

Matthew 5:13-15

1 Peter 3:15

CONCLUSION

In John 1:12, we are reminded that through Christ, we are given the right to be called children of God. God is our father and we are heirs with Christ and we share in His glory. Our identity in Christ is forever to be our primary identifier. We are not fathers, mothers, plumbers, or accountants first; we are Christians first. I am Christian, first.

For me, being Christian first involves the willingness, determination, and ability to consistently place God at the forefront of my life so I can experience the fullness of His plan for me—and so I can help effect change in the lives of others. As the stories in this book illustrate, there is nothing simple about such a lofty goal.

It has been difficult and daunting to navigate my way through life knowing that even though I live in this world I am not of it. The tension between these two realities—between these two worlds—informs my passion to carry the kingdom of God on Earth into our professional lives and compelled me to write this book.

After all, I realize this tension isn't exclusive to me. Throughout the Bible, God's people have struggled with balancing their God-given identities with their "professional" identities. In the Old Testament, leaders like David, Moses, Elijah, and Daniel embraced that moment of clarity when they became all-in for God. In the New Testament, when Christianity sparked in the first century and certain death loomed around every corner, the new band of brothers and sisters called "Christians" would also have to decide if they would stand with and for Jesus, regardless of the cost.

There should be no separation between who we are in Christ and who we are in the world. In a society in which God is systematically being forced out of schools, government, and the workplace, it is our responsibility to bring Christ back into the world in these key areas—especially where we work. At the end of the day, this is where we spend most of our time and the majority of our waking hours. Where we typically interact with many others. Where we wield the influence God has given us.

In the last chapter, I talked about being a "closet Christian." We can't do it anymore. We can't afford to. Not now. In this era of confusion, fear, political and cultural unrest, we are to be the salt and light of this world. We must be willing to do those things that others are not willing to do if we are to be successful in advancing God's kingdom here on Earth. Yes, that includes continuing to be good neighbors, trusted friends, and reliable workers—but we are Christians first.

Experiencing success as a Christian in the workplace today requires temerity, patience, and godly discernment—and that can require quite a balancing act. We need to be unwaveringly bold, but not obnoxiously overbearing. We need to be lovingly patient, but expect timely results. We need to follow God's leading, but respect the journeys of colleagues who don't have a relationship with Him yet. These realities can muddy the waters if we allow them to, and distract from our original intent: to show the world what a person looks like who puts Christ first in everything they do.

God has His reasons for uniquely calling us and placing us in positions of influence and, sometimes, even power. My hope and prayer for you, dear reader, is that you will take seriously the opportunities God has placed in your professional life and that you will incorporate the wisdom He has lovingly passed down through the ages. I pray that the examples of Esther, John the Baptist, Joseph, and many others contained in the pages of this book will give you strength and confidence as you move forward in your work-faith integration.

Most importantly, I pray that in everything you do you'll keep in mind that, above all else, you're a Christian first.

PRAYER OF SALVATION

If you don't know Jesus Christ, you can start a new life by accepting Him into your heart today.

Heavenly Father, I am a sinner and I have fallen short of the glory of God — please forgive me for my sins. Even in my weakness, you continue to demonstrate your love for me by sending your Son, Jesus, to die for me so that I may have your gift of eternal life through Jesus Christ our Lord. Your Word says that "Whoever calls on the name of the LORD shall be saved." I am calling upon you, Lord, and I am confessing right now with my mouth the Lord Jesus. I believe in my heart that you, my loving God, have raised Him from the dead, and I will be saved.

Thank you for loving me and choosing me, Lord. I am no longer the same person but now I am renewed, for it is by grace I have been saved. I will boldly confess before all that Jesus Christ is my Lord and Savior and I am prepared to do the good works for the kingdom of God that you have already prepared for me to do.

Amen!

If you've prayed this prayer and have accepted Jesus Christ as your Lord and Savior, please drop me a note and share your story so that I may pray for you and celebrate your new life in Christ Jesus.

Scripture References

Romans 3:23

Romans 5:8

Romans 6:23

Acts 2:21

Romans 10:9

Matthew 10:32

2 Corinthians 5:17

Ephesians 2:8-10

ABOUT THE AUTHOR

Dr. Grace Alexis Stephens is currently Chancellor of MacCormac College where she served as one of the youngest college presidents in America. She is the first woman to hold the presidency post at this 115-year old institution. Prior to joining MacCormac, Stephens concurrently held positions at Duke University as Associate Dean for Undergraduate Education and as Executive Director of the Comprehensive Education Institute for Duke University Health System.

Over the past 30 years, Stephens has held senior leadership positions at several of this country's major research institutions. She also worked as an executive level business developer and profit and loss manager for Kaplan, Inc. and as a business relationship manager for Goldman Sachs & Co. on Wall Street. These unique experiences have positioned her as a leader and innovator in academia and business.

A native New Yorker, Stephens received her B.A. from the State University of New York; an M.A. from New York University; an Ed.M. from Columbia University; an Ed.D. from the University of Pennsylvania; and she studied at the Institute for Higher Education at Harvard University. She is a licensed minister and holds ministry credentials at the doctoral level from seminary.

Stephens is America's leading advisor to Christian professionals. She is a motivational speaker, lecturer, entrepreneur, business and ministry consultant. Grace is a published researcher and author who writes, speaks, and advises on academic management, business strategy, fund development, and Christian topics. She is the founder of The Global Christian Professional Women's Association – the world's largest and premier resource in serving and advancing professional women of faith.

You can invite Grace Stephens to speak at your next ministry event or business conference or follow her online at **GraceStephens.org**